Mastering HTML5 Forms

Create dynamic and responsive web forms with this
in- depth, hands-on guide

Gaurav Gupta

BIRMINGHAM - MUMBAI

Mastering HTML5 Forms

First published: November 2013

Production Reference: 1151113

Published by Packt Publishing Ltd.

Livery Place
35 Livery Street
Birmingham B3 2PB, UK.

ISBN 978-1-78216-466-1

www.packtpub.com

Cover Image by Aniket Sawant (aniket_sawant_photography@hotmail.com)

Credits

Author
Gaurav Gupta

Reviewers
Errietta Kostala

Sulek Shrikrishna Mulay

Acquisition Editor
Nikhil Chinnari

Lead Technical Editor
Shaon Basu

Technical Editors
Pooja Nair

Harshad Vairat

Copy Editors
Mradula Hegde

Roshni Banerjee

Dipti Kapadia

Aditi Shetty

Project Coordinator
Joel Goveya

Proofreader
Paul Hindle

Indexer
Rekha Nair

Production Coordinator
Adonia Jones

Cover Work
Adonia Jones

About the Author

Gaurav Gupta is a budding, young IT professional with a large amount of exposure working on web and cross-platform application development. He is a versatile developer and is always keen to learn new technologies that are updated in this domain. His passion for his work makes him stand apart from other developers.

A graduate in Computer Science, he currently works for a reputed CMMI Level 5 company and has developed several web and mobile applications for internal use.

Gaurav is a native of Chandigarh, India, and he currently lives in Pune, India.

First of all I would like to thank the almighty and my family, who have always guided me to walk on the right path in life. I acknowledge, with a deep sense of gratitude and most sincere appreciation, the valuable guidance and unfailing encouragement rendered to me by Mr. Arjun Gupta. I would like to thank him for his proficient, enthusiastic guidance, useful encouragement, and immense help.

I would also like to thank Miss. Sulek Shrikrishna Mulay for being an amazing teacher and guide and for taking pains to technically review this book.

I wish to extend my sincere gratitude to Aurita, Yogesh, and Joel from Packt Publishing for their guidance and valuable suggestions, which proved extremely useful and helpful in the completion of this book. My heartfelt gratitude and indebtedness goes to all those people in my life who gave me constructive criticism, as it contributed directly or indirectly in a significant way towards the completion of this book. My special thanks goes to my friend Raghav and my colleagues, especially Vikas, Shreshtha, Arup, Abhishek, and Sameer, for their support and encouragement, which has been a constant source of assurance, guidance, strength, and inspection to me.

About the Reviewers

Errietta Kostala is a web developer who is currently studying at the University of Huddersfield in the UK. Having worked on several websites and applications in the past few years and having been actively contributing to open source software, Errietta has a vast background in both client-side and server-side web programming languages.

I would like to thank the author and publishers for giving me the opportunity to review this book. In addition to this, I would like to thank my University and the open source community for giving me the knowledge and experience needed to do this.

Sulek Shrikrishna Mulay is a BE in Information Technology. She has around 8 years of experience in the IT industry. She currently works for a reputed CMMI Level 5 company.

She has technical expertise in Java/J2EE (Struts Framework) and cross-platform applications (Android/iOS) with HTML5/jQuery/JavaScript/jQueryMobile/Sencha Touch/Phonegap (Cordova) technologies.

She has also received many awards for technical expertise and extracurricular activities.

Sulek is a native of Solapur, Maharashtra, India, and currently lives in Pune, India.

I would like to thank my parents, Shrikrishna D Mulay and Nutan S Mulay, for their immense support. I also want to thank my sister Sneha Mulay and my brother Harshwardhan Mulay for always being there for me.

www.PacktPub.com

Support files, eBooks, discount offers and more

You might want to visit www.PacktPub.com for support files and downloads related to your book.

Did you know that Packt offers eBook versions of every book published, with PDF and ePub files available? You can upgrade to the eBook version at www.PacktPub.com and as a print book customer, you are entitled to a discount on the eBook copy. Get in touch with us at service@packtpub.com for more details.

At www.PacktPub.com, you can also read a collection of free technical articles, sign up for a range of free newsletters and receive exclusive discounts and offers on Packt books and eBooks.

http://PacktLib.PacktPub.com

Do you need instant solutions to your IT questions? PacktLib is Packt's online digital book library. Here, you can access, read and search across Packt's entire library of books.

Why Subscribe?
- Fully searchable across every book published by Packt
- Copy and paste, print and bookmark content
- On demand and accessible via web browser

Free Access for Packt account holders

If you have an account with Packt at www.PacktPub.com, you can use this to access PacktLib today and view nine entirely free books. Simply use your login credentials for immediate access.

Table of Contents

Preface

Web viewers may never know about the background of an application, such as HTML5, CSS3, Responsive Web Design, or PHP. What they want to know is whether your application works on their device or not and how much effort is required.

Even though web development has changed over the years, the core task of creating a web page has not been changed. We create a document and put it out on the Web for people to view. To put something on the Web, we need to learn some special languages that are accepted on the Web. Yes, we are talking about the scripting languages such as HTML and PHP.

The main objective of this book is to ensure that the user who fills the form built by you should enjoy and feel satisfied in every possible way. Here, satisfaction means the look and feel of the forms and minimum adjustments on the page while navigating, which can be on a desktop computer, mobile device, or mini laptop.

This book has been written keeping in mind that readers should enjoy a step-by-step, example driven, and visual-based approach to learning. This book will cover many aspects of web development, such as the language used to develop the web forms as well as ways to make web forms look good and accept information from visitors.

This book will act as a platform with which you will learn how to create beautiful and responsive forms and link them to the database where the form information will be stored.

What this book covers

Chapter 1, Forms and Their Significance, explains what web forms are and how we can create these using the new HTML5 form elements. It also explains the benefits of web forms along with the guidelines that must always be kept in mind while designing and developing a form.

Chapter 2, Validations of Forms, explains validations and their necessity in forms as well as the new HTML5 elements and their attributes that reduce the effort of client-side validations. It gives a brief description of the validation constraints and supported API's and also briefs us on the customization of error messages on the browser.

Chapter 3, Styling the Forms, explains the CSS3 properties that can be utilized to make forms more presentable. It details us about the vendor-specific prefixes that are utilized in different browsers along with the effective styling guidelines that must be kept in mind while enhancing the look and feel of a form.

Chapter 4, Connection with Database, explains briefly about linking a form to the server using PHP and MySQL, which are used by web developers to store user information.

Chapter 5, Responsive Web Forms, explains responsive designing and approaches that can be used to make our form responsive. It also discusses the guidelines you should follow to make a responsive form.

What you need for this book

Any text editor such as Notepad++ or Bluefish can be used to write HTML and JavaScript code. In Windows, Notepad can also be used to create a simple HTML file and CSS and JavaScript code can be embedded inside it, which can then be opened in a web browser.

The good news is that almost every web browser comes with a built-in HTML and JavaScript Interpreter that compiles the code and executes it within the web browser host environment during run-time.

PHP files can be written in any of the editors used for writing HTML, CSS, or JavaScript. For linking the form to the server, the Wamp server is used in Windows and phpMyAdmin tool is used for MySQL databases.

Who this book is for

This book will help anyone who is willing to enhance their skills in building web forms using HTML5 and related technologies.

This book should be read by those who are interested in learning how HTML5, CSS3, and PHP can be used to build responsive, beautiful, and dynamic web forms.

Different readers will find different parts of the book interesting.

Without worrying much about having in-depth knowledge of previous W3C specifications and PHP, users who have learned HTML and PHP on a beginner level can directly learn how to build web forms using HTML5, CSS3, and PHP and collect customer information.

Conventions

In this book, you will find a number of styles of text that distinguish between different kinds of information. Here are some examples of these styles, and an explanation of their meaning.

Code words in text, database table names, folder names, filenames, file extensions, pathnames, dummy URLs, user input, and Twitter handles are shown as follows: "We can include other contexts through the use of the include directive."

A block of code is set as follows:

```
<div class="gender">
  <label for="gender">Gender</label><br>
  <input type="radio" name="gender"><label>Male</label>
  <input type="radio" name="gender"><label>Female</label>
</div><br>
```

When we wish to draw your attention to a particular part of a code block, the relevant lines or items are set in bold:

```
font-family: Helvetica, Arial, sans-serif;
  color: #000000;
  background: rgba(212,228,239,1);
  background: -moz-linear-gradient(top, rgba(212,228,239,1) 0%,
    rgba(134,174,204,1) 100%);
  background: -webkit-gradient(left top, left bottom, color-
    stop(0%, rgba(212,228,239,1)), color-stop(100%,
    rgba(134,174,204,1)));
```

New terms and **important words** are shown in bold. Words that you see on the screen, in menus or dialog boxes for example, appear in the text like this: " For submitting the form to the server, we have created a **Submit** button".

In this book, we have used 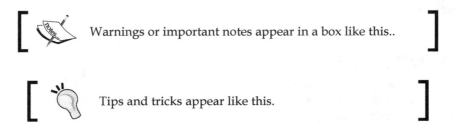 for Mozilla Firefox, Google Chrome, Safari, Internet Explorer, and Opera.

> Warnings or important notes appear in a box like this..

> Tips and tricks appear like this.

Reader feedback

Feedback from our readers is always welcome. Let us know what you think about this book—what you liked or may have disliked. Reader feedback is important for us to develop titles that you really get the most out of.

To send us general feedback, simply send an e-mail to feedback@packtpub.com, and mention the book title via the subject of your message.

If there is a topic that you have expertise in and you are interested in either writing or contributing to a book, see our author guide on www.packtpub.com/authors.

Customer support

Now that you are the proud owner of a Packt book, we have a number of things to help you to get the most from your purchase.

Downloading the example code

You can download the example code files for all Packt books you have purchased from your account at http://www.packtpub.com. If you purchased this book elsewhere, you can visit http://www.packtpub.com/support and register to have the files e-mailed directly to you.

Errata

Although we have taken every care to ensure the accuracy of our content, mistakes do happen. If you find a mistake in one of our books—maybe a mistake in the text or the code—we would be grateful if you would report this to us. By doing so, you can save other readers from frustration and help us improve subsequent versions of this book. If you find any errata, please report them by visiting http://www.packtpub.com/submit-errata, selecting your book, clicking on the **errata submission form** link, and entering the details of your errata. Once your errata are verified, your submission will be accepted and the errata will be uploaded on our website, or added to any list of existing errata, under the Errata section of that title. Any existing errata can be viewed by selecting your title from http://www.packtpub.com/support.

Piracy

Piracy of copyright material on the Internet is an ongoing problem across all media. At Packt, we take the protection of our copyright and licenses very seriously. If you come across any illegal copies of our works, in any form, on the Internet, please provide us with the location address or website name immediately so that we can pursue a remedy.

Please contact us at copyright@packtpub.com with a link to the suspected pirated material.

We appreciate your help in protecting our authors, and our ability to bring you valuable content.

Questions

You can contact us at questions@packtpub.com if you are having a problem with any aspect of the book, and we will do our best to address it.

Forms and Their Significance

1

Using forms in a web page is the most effective way to gather relevant data from the user. Forms are how users really interact with the application whether it's a search form, a login screen, or a multipage registration wizard. Forms can have inputs such as name, gender, credit card number, password, images, or upload files into the forms.

In this chapter we will cover the following topics:

- Web forms and their benefits
- The new HTML5 `<form>` elements
- Building a web form
- Guidelines to build a web form

Understanding web forms

Before we start learning about HTML5 forms, let us understand what a web form is.

Forms on a web page provide an interface where information can be shared between a client and a user more easily and securely in comparison to paper-based forms. They are a collection of various `<input>` types, such as `textbox`, `radiobutton`, and `checkbox`, which allow users to perform various actions and simplifies decision making.

Forms have always been a fundamental part of the Web. Without them, various web transactions, discussions, and efficient searches would simply not be possible. Web-based forms are supported in most browsers and can be used to give feedback after purchasing a product, retrieve search results from a search engine, contact for any service, and much more.

With a simple example, let us understand what a web form is. Say you once went to a hospital and the receptionist gave you a printed form to fill out. You would have come across many fields that collect information about a patient. Some of them asked you to write the patient's name and address in what looked like a textbox or a text area, and other details such as type of room and so on; you were also asked to choose one or multiple radio buttons or checkboxes from the options. The same concept follows for HTML5 forms. You have to fill out the fields of that form and press a button to send this information to the server, rather than going to the hospital and handing the form over to the receptionist.

Benefits

Forms in web pages offer plenty of advantages over paper-based forms. Apart from being used to gather data online, web forms offer convenience and speed for both the user and the form owner.

Some advantages of web forms are:

- Online forms help the customers to talk to the companies as they contain digitally stored data and deduce that data to meaningful information
- The form owners can quickly build and distribute the HTML5 interface, targeting a large audience
- The form owner can easily update and modify forms as needed
- The Cascading Style Sheets (CSS) and JavaScript attributes allow authors to customize form controls with specific styles and functions
- Web forms are time saving and cost effective as they require no manpower to gather information
- They provide a visibility for decision making, for example, shopping online on websites such as eBay
- As the data is entered directly by the customer,it can be easily sorted to get the required information

Even if forms have many benefits, building them is not the nicest job and can become a headache as some forms can get very complicated if we talk about validation, error handling, and styling. We either validate or catch the errors using a server-side language or we use JavaScript, or even both. Whichever the case, the web forms can take up a lot of your development time and this can be a problem. With HTML5, however, some of this pain has been taken away by the introduction of the new `<form>` types, which we can use.

In spite of many enhancements in HTML5, some things are kept the same such as:

- Forms still send the values to the server when the user clicks on the **Submit** button
- Forms are still enclosed in the `<form>` element, as shown in the following code snippet:

```
<form action= "#">
  <input type= "text" name= "emailaddress">
  <input type= "submit" name= "submit">
</form>
```

- Form controls are still fully scriptable

However, for the HTML5 forms, there is no need to enclose the `<form>` controls in the `<form>` element.

HTML versus HTML5 forms

An HTML5 form provides two major advantages over previous versions. They are:

- Tedious scripting and styling of forms that was required in earlier versions of HTML was removed because HTML5's new `<form>` types and inbuilt validations takes semantic markup to the next level
- Even if scripting is disabled in the browser, users can experience the benefits of HTML5 forms

The form `<input>` types, elements, and attributes

The HTML5 forms focus on enhancing the existing simple HTML forms to encompass more types of controls and address the limitations that web developers face today. One of the best things about them is that you can use almost all the new input types, elements, and attributes right now and the HTML5 forms are fully backward compatible. The browser, which supports the new HTML5 elements, enhances their features, otherwise the browser, which does not support it, displays them as a textbox.

In this section, we will learn the new HTML5 `<form>` elements, such as the `<input>` types, elements, and attributes that are introduced to enhance the capabilities of forms.

The <form> <input> types

- `date`: The `date` type allows the user to select a date with no time zone.

  It is supported in .

  Syntax:

  ```
  <input type= "date" name= "#">
  ```

  Attributes:

  - `value`: The initial value. The format is yyyy-mm-dd
  - `min`, `max`: The range in which the smallest and largest dates can be selected

- `datetime`: The `datetime` type allows the user to select a date and a time with the time zone set to UTC.

  The format is yyyy-mm-dd HH:MM.

  It is supported in .

  Syntax:

  ```
  <input type= "datetime" name= "#">
  ```

- `datetime-local`: The `datetime-local` type allows the user to select a date and time with no time zone. The format used is yyyy-mm-dd HH:MM.

  It is supported in .

  Syntax:

  ```
  <input type= "datetime-local" name= "#">
  ```

- `color`: The `color` type results in opening a color chooser pop up and is used to choose a color of the `<input>` type #rrggbb (hex value). It could be represented by a swatch or a wheel picker.

  The value chosen must be a valid simple color's hex value such as #ffffff.

  It is supported in .

  Syntax:

  ```
  <input type= "color" id= "#"name= "#">
  ```

Attributes:

- º   `value`: The initial value

- `number`: The `number` type allows the user to input the numbers in either `integer` or `floating point`.

  It is also called a spinner.

  We can set restrictions on what numbers are accepted.

  It is supported in .

  Syntax:

  ```
  <input type= "number" name= "#">
  ```

  Attributes:

  - º   `value`: The initial value
  - º   `min`, `max`: The range in which the smallest and largest values can be selected with the up/down arrows
  - º   `step`: This tells us how much to change the values when we scroll the spinner

- `range`: The `range` type allows the user to input the numbers in either integer or floating point from a range of numbers. It is displayed in the form of a slider.

  Using this, the exact value is not shown unless you use JavaScript, so use `<input type="number" />` if you want the user to choose an exact value.

  We can set restrictions on what numbers are accepted.

  It is supported in .

  Syntax:

  ```
  <input type= "range" name= "#">
  ```

  Attributes:

  - º   `value`: The initial value. The default value is the mid of the slider.
  - º   `min`, `max`: The range in which the smallest and largest values can be selected. The default for min is 0 and max is 100.
  - º   `step`: This tells us how much to change the values when we scroll the spinner. The default is 1.

- email: The email type allows the user to enter the text in e-mail address format email@example.com.

   The entered text is automatically validated when clicked on the **Submit** button.

   If multiple attributes are specified, multiple e-mail addresses can be entered, separated by commas.

   It is supported in 🌐 🌐 🌐 🌐.

   Syntax:

   ```
   <input type= "email" name= "#">
   ```

   Attributes:

   - value: The initial value (a legal e-mail address)

   Using multiple attributes, that is, more than one e-mail ID, is accepted and each attribute is separated by a comma.

- search: The <input> type search allows the user to enter text that the user wants to search for.

   A search field behaves like a standard text field and has inbuilt clear text functionality, such as the cross button in WebKit browsers.

   It is supported in 🌐 🌐 🌐 .

   Syntax:

   ```
   <input type= "search" name= "#">
   ```

   Attributes:

   - value: The initial value

- tel: The tel type allows the user to input a telephone number. tel does not provide any default syntax, so if you want to ensure a particular format, you can use pattern to do additional validation.

   No browser support till now.

   Syntax:

   ```
   <input type= "tel" name= "#">
   ```

   Attributes:

   - value: The initial value as a phone number

- month: The month type allows the user to select a month and a year with no time zone.

  It is supported in ⊚ ◯ ⊚.

  Syntax:

  ```
  <input type= "month" name= "#" >
  ```

  Attributes:

  - value: The initial value. The format is yyyy-mm.
  - min, max: The range in which the smallest and largest values can be selected.

- time: The time type allows the user to select a time value with hour, minutes, seconds, and fractional seconds with no time zone.

  It is supported in ⊚ ⊚ ◯.

  Syntax:

  ```
  <input type= "time" name= "#">
  ```

- url: The url type allows the user to input an absolute URL.

  The entered text is automatically validated when clicked on the **Submit** button.

  It is supported in ⊚ ⊚ ⊚ ◯.

  Syntax:

  ```
  <input type= "url" name= "#" >
  ```

  Attributes:

  - value: The initial value as an absolute URL

- week: The week type allows the user to select a week and a year with no time zone.

  It is supported in ◯ ⊚ ⊚ ⊚.

  Syntax:

  ```
  <input type= "week" name= "#">
  ```

  Attributes:

  - value: The initial value. The format is yyyy-mmW.

So far we have learned about the various <input> types. Now let's see the new HTML5 <form> elements.

The <form> elements

- <datalist>: The <datalist> element provides a list of predefined options for form controls to the user as they input data. It is used to provide an autocomplete feature on the <form> elements.

  For instance, if a user enters some text in a text field, a list would drop down with prefilled values that they could choose from.

  It is supported in .

  For example:

```
<input list= "browsers" name= "browser">
<datalist id= "browsers">
  <option value= "Internet Explorer">
  <option value= "Firefox">
</datalist>
```

- <keygen>: The <keygen> element is used to provide a secure way to authenticate users.

  When the form is submitted, the private key is stored in the local keystore and the public key is packaged and sent to the server.

  It is supported in   .

  For example:

```
<form action= "keygen.html" method= "get">
  <input type= "text" name= "username">
  <keygen name= "security">
  <input type= "submit">
</form>
```

- <output>: The <output> element represents the result of a calculation performed like the one performed by scripts.

  It is supported in .

  For example:

```
<form onsubmit="return false"
  oninput="o.value=parseInt(a.value)+parseInt(b.value)">
  <input name="a" type="number" step="any">+
  <input name="b" type="number" step= "any">
=<output name="o"></output>
</form>
```

Now let us see the new HTML5 <form> attributes.

The <form> attributes

- autocomplete: The autocomplete attribute allows users to complete the forms based on earlier inputs. We can have an autocomplete on option for the form and an off option for specific input fields or vice versa.

  It works with both the <form> and <input> types such as textbox, datepicker, range, color, url, tel, search, and email.

  It is supported in .

  For example:

  ```
  <input type="text" name="city" autocomplete="on">
  ```

- autofocus: When the autofocus attribute is added, an <input>type automatically gets focus when the page loads.

  For instance, when we open the Google home page or any search engine, the focus automatically goes to the textbox where a user enters the text to perform a search.

  It works with the <input> types, textbox, search, url, email, tel, and password.

  It is supported in .

  For example:

  ```
  <input type="text" name="city">
  <input type="text" name="state" autofocus>
  ```

- placeholder: The placeholder attribute gives users a hint that describes the expected value of an <input> field.

  It disappears when the control is clicked on or gains focus.

  It should be used only for short descriptions or else use the title attribute.

  It works with the <input> types, textbox, search, url, email, tel, and password.

  It is supported in .

  For example:

  ```
  <input type="text" name="name" placeholder="First Name">
  ```

- `min` and `max`: The `min` and `max` attributes are used to specify the minimum and maximum value to an `<input>` type.

  It works with the `<input>` types, `number`, `range`, `date`, `datetime`, `datetime-local`, `month`, `time`, and `week`.

  It is supported in 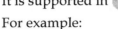.

  For example:

  ```
  <input type="number" min="1" max="5">
  ```

- `list`: The `list` attribute refers to a `<datalist>` element that contains predefined options for an `<input>` element.

  It is used to provide an `autocomplete` feature on the `<form>`elements.

  For instance, if a user enters some text in a text field, a list would drop down with prefilled values from which they could choose.

  It works with the `<input>` types, `textbox`, `search`, `url`, `email`, `tel`.

  It is supported in .

  For example:

  ```
  <input list= "browsers" name= "browser">
  <datalist id= "browsers">
    <option value= "Internet Explorer">
    <option value= "Firefox">
  </datalist>
  ```

- `formnovalidate`: The `formnovalidate` attribute specifies that the form should not be validated during submission. It overrides the `novalidate` attribute of the `<form>`elements.

  It works with the `<input>` types, `submit` and `image`.

  It is supported in .

  For example:

  ```
  <input type="email" name="email">
  <input type="submit" formnovalidate value="Submit">
  ```

- `form`: The `form` attribute specifies one or more forms that an `<input>` type belongs to, or in other words, it allows the users to associate any orphaned form control with any `<form>` element on the page.

  It is supported in .

  For example:

```
<body>
  <form action="form.html" id="form1">
    <input type="text" name="fname"><br>
    <input type="submit" value="Submit">
  </form>
  <p>The "Last name" field below is outside the form
    element, but it is still a part of the form</p>
  <input type="text" name="lname" form="form1">
</body>
```

- `formaction`: The `formaction` attribute specifies the URL of a file or application that will submit the form.

  It works with the `<input>` types, `submit` and `image`.

  It is supported in .

  For example:

```
<input type="submit" value="Submit" formaction="form.html">
```

- `formenctype`: The `formenctype` attribute specifies how the form data is encoded when submitting to the server.

  It works with the `post` method only.

  It works with the `<input>` types, `submit` and `image`.

  It is supported in .

  For example:

```
<input type="submit" value="Submit"
  formenctype="multipart/form-data">
```

- `formmethod`: The `formmethod` attribute specifies which HTTP method such as GET, POST, PUT, and DELETE will be used to submit the form data.

  It works with the `<input>` types, `submit` and `image`.

  It is supported in ⬤◐⬤◐⬤.

  For example:

  ```
  <input type="submit" value="Submit" formmethod="post">
  ```

- `formtarget`: The `formtarget` attribute specifies the target window to display the response received after submitting the form.

  It works with the `<input>` types, `submit` and `image`.

  It is supported in ⬤◐⬤◐⬤.

  For example:

  ```
  <input type="submit" value="Submit" formtarget="_self">
  ```

  Values:

  ○ `blank`

  ○ `self`

  ○ `parent`

  ○ `top`

  ○ `framename`

- `multiple`: The `multiple` attribute allows users to enter more than one value to the `<input>` types.

  It works with the `<input>` types, `email` and `file`.

  It is supported in ⬤◐⬤◐⬤.

  For example:

  ```
  <input type= "file" name= "image"multiple>
  ```

- `novalidate`: The `novalidate` attribute specifies that the form should not be validated when the **Submit** button is clicked.

  It is supported in .

  For example:

```
<form action= "form.html" novalidate>
  <input type= "text" name= "city">
  <input type= "text" name= "state" autofocus>
</form>
```

- `step`: Let us understand the `step` attribute with an example. If `step= 2`, legal numbers could be 2, 0, 2, 4, and 6.

  It works with the `<input>` types, `number`, `range`, `date`, `datetime`, `datetime-local`, `month`, `time`, and `week`.

  It is supported in .

  For example:

```
<input type= "range" name= "#" step= "2">
```

- `required`: The `required` attribute, when added, enforces that an input field must be filled out before submitting the form.

  Currently, the error messages are specific to the browsers and cannot be controlled by the CSS.

  It replaces the basic `<form>` validations that were implemented with JavaScript, thus saving development time.

  It is supported in .

  For example:

```
<input type= "text" name= "city"required>
```

- `pattern`: Using the `pattern` attribute, you can declare your own requirements for validation using `Regular Expressions` (regex).

  It works with the `<input>` types, `text`, `search`, `url`, `tel`, `email`, and `password`.

In case, the value entered by a user does not match the pattern, it will display a browser generic message.

It is supported in ⬤⬤⬤⬤.

For example:

```
<input type= "text" name= "country_code" pattern= "[A-Za-
    z]{3}" placeholder= "Three letter country code">
```

Building an HTML5 form

So far, what we have learned about HTML5 forms is only theoretical, but now it's time to take this learning to the next level. Taking it to the next level means that in this section, we will build a sample form with some understanding of how they are structured and the new <form> types, which we have already discussed.

Here we will spend less time on styling or functionality such as design and validations but more on the core of the new <form> types of HTML5. This form is best supported in browsers that support HTML5 features.

In this example, we will build a health survey form.

This example demonstrates a simple form, using basic HTML elements and new <form> elements, and the code should be self-explanatory.

Now, let us take a look at the code. The following code is the CSS of the form and is maintained in a separate file with a .css extension (external CSS file), which is linked to the main HTML page. Having a separate CSS file is also a good practice.

```
html {
  background-color: #333;
  margin: 0px;
  padding: 0px;
}
body {
  font-size:12px;
  width: 517px;
  padding: 20px;
  margin: 10px auto;
  background-color: #eee;
  font-family: Helvetica, Arial, sans-serif;
  color: #333;
}
```

```
label{
  font-weight:bold;
}

/* General Form */
.heading{
  font-size:20px;
}
.gender{
  position:relative;
  top:-42px;
  left:185px;
}
.selectOption{
  width:239px;
}
.textboxAddress{
  width:474px;
}
.textboxAddressDetail{
  width:232px;
}
.legend{
  font-weight:bold;
  font-size:14px;
}
.submit{
  text-align:center;
}
```

The following code is the main HTML page in which we built the structure of the form. The `<fieldset>` tags are enclosed within the `<form>` tag.

The structure is broken into sections for better understanding. Moreover, the `<form>` types are highlighted in bold.

The following is a code snippet for displaying a form for personal information:

```
<fieldset>
  <legend class="legend">Personal Information</legend>
  <div>
    <label for="name">Name</label><br>
    <input type="text" placeholder="First" autofocus>
    <input type="text" placeholder="Last">
  </div><br>
```

```
<div>
  <label for="dob">Date of Birth</label><br>
  <input type="date" value="">
</div>
<div class="gender">
  <label for="gender">Gender</label><br>
  <input type="radio" name="gender"><label>Male</label>
  <input type="radio" name="gender"><label>Female</label>
</div><br>
<div>
  <label for="address">Address</label><br>
  <input type="text" class="textboxAddress" placeholder="Street
    Address"><br>
  <input type="text" class="textboxAddress" placeholder="Address
    Line 2"><br>
  <input type="text" class="textboxAddressDetail"
    placeholder="City">
  <input type="text" class="textboxAddressDetail"
    placeholder="State/Province"><br>
  <input type="text" class="textboxAddressDetail"
    placeholder="Pincode">
  <select class="selectOption">
    <option value="Country">Select Country</option>
  </select>
</div><br>
<div>
  <label for="contact">Phone Number</label><br>
  <input type="tel" class="textboxAddressDetail"
    placeholder="Home">
  <input type="tel" class="textboxAddressDetail"
    placeholder="Work">
</div><br>
<div>
  <label for="email">Email Address</label><br>
  <input type="email" class="textboxAddressDetail"
    placeholder="email@example.com">
</div>
</fieldset>
```

The output of the code is as follows:

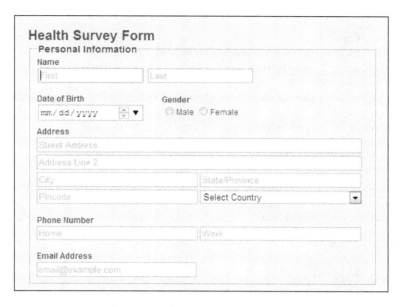

This section asks the respondents about their personal information such as name, address, and other details. We have used `<label>` with descriptive text and tied it to the form control.

We have also used the `autofocus` attribute on the first textbox so that an `<input>` element automatically gets focus when the page loads. The `placeholder` attribute is used several times in the first textbox as `First` to give a hint to the respondents of what is required as content. For date of birth, we have used the `<input>` type `date`, which opens as a calendar.

The basic HTML elements' `<input>` types, such as `radiobutton`, `textbox`, and the drop-down list have also been used.

Similarly, for the phone number field, the `<input>` type `tel` is used, and for the e-mail address field the `<input>` type `email` is used.

The following is a code snippet for displaying a general information form:

```
<fieldset>
  <legend class="legend">General Information</legend>
  <div>
    <label for="info">What is your</label><br>
    <input type="text" placeholder="Age?">
    <input type="text" placeholder="Weight?">
```

```
      <input type="text" placeholder="Height?">
</div><br>
<div>
   <label for="exerciceinfo">Do you regularly engage in any of
      the following exercises?</label><br>
   <div><input type="checkbox" name="smoke"><label>Walking
      </label><br>
   <input type="checkbox" name="smoke"><label>Running</label>
      </div>
   <div><input type="checkbox" name="smoke"><label>Swimming
      </label><br>
   <input type="checkbox" name="smoke"><label>Biking
      </label></div>
   <div><input type="checkbox" name="smoke"><label>Others
      </label><br>
   <input type="checkbox" name="smoke"><label>I don't exercise
      </label></div>
</div><br>
<div>
   <label for="sleep">On average, how many hours a day do you
      sleep?</label><br>
   <input type="number" class="textboxAddressDetail">
</div><br>
<div>
   <label for="smoking">Have you ever smoked cigarettes, pipes or
      cigars?</label><br>
   <input type="radio" name="smoke"><label>Yes</label>
   <input type="radio" name="smoke"><label>No</label>
</div><br>
<div>
   <label for="drugs">Are you currently using or do you have a
      history of illegal drug use?</label><br>
   <input type="radio" name="drugs"><label>Yes</label>
   <input type="radio" name="drugs"><label>No</label>
</div><br>
<div>
   <label for="alcohol">Do you consume alcohol?</label><br>
   <input type="radio" name="alcohol"><label>Yes</label>
   <input type="radio" name="alcohol"><label>No</label>
</div>
</fieldset>
```

The output of the code is as follows:

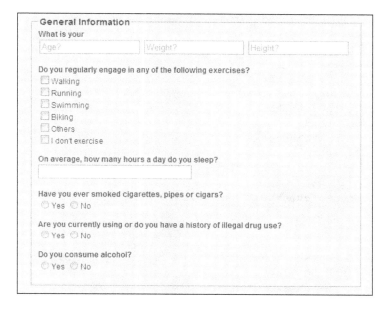

The top section of the form asks the respondents about general information, such as age, weight, height, and other information about their daily routine.

Here, we have used basic HTML `<form>` `<input>` types, such as textbox, radiobutton, and checkbox along with the new `<form>` attributes such as placeholder, for taking the inputs from the respondent.

The following code snippet displays a form to store medical information:

```
<fieldset>
  <legend class="legend">Medical Information</legend>
  <div>
    <label for= "disease">Check all that apply to you or your
      immediate family?</label><br>
    <input type="checkbox" name="disease"><label>Asthma
      </label><br>
    <input type="checkbox" name="disease"><label>Cancer
      </label><br>
    <input type="checkbox" name="disease"><label>HIV and AIDS
      </label><br>
    <input type="checkbox" name="disease"><label>Diabetes
      </label><br>
```

```
    <input type="checkbox" name="disease"><label>Hypertension
    </label><br>
    <input type="checkbox" name="disease"><label>Malaria
    </label><br>
    <input type="checkbox" name="disease"><label>Seizure Disorder
    </label><br>
    <input type="checkbox" name="disease"><label>Psychiatric
    Disorders</label><br>
    <input type="checkbox" name="disease"><label>Mental Health
    </label><br>
    <input type="checkbox" name="disease"><label>Stroke
    </label><br>
    <input type="checkbox" name="disease"><label>Others
    </label><br>
    <input type="checkbox" name="disease"><label>Not Applicable
    </label>
</div><br>
<div>
    <label for= "symptons">Checkall symptoms you are currently
    experiencing</label><br>
    <input type="checkbox" name="symptoms"><label>Allergy
    </label><br>
    <input type="checkbox" name="symptoms"><label>Eye</label><br>
    <input type="checkbox" name="symptoms"><label>Lymphatic
    </label><br>
    <input type="checkbox" name="symptoms"><label>Fever
    </label><br>
    <input type="checkbox" name="symptoms"><label>Eating Disorder
    </label><br>
    <input type="checkbox" name="symptoms"><label>Hemtalogical
    </label><br>
    <input type="checkbox" name="symptoms"><label>Musculoskeletal
    Pain</label><br>
    <input type="checkbox" name="symptoms"><label>Skin</label><br>
    <input type="checkbox" name="symptoms"><label>Gastrointestinal
    </label><br>
    <input type="checkbox" name="symptoms"><label>Weight Loss
    </label><br>
    <input type="checkbox" name="symptoms"><label>Others
    </label><br>
    <input type="checkbox" name="symptoms"><label>Not Applicable
    </label>
</div><br>
<div>
```

```
        <label for="allergy">Please list any medication allergies that
          you have</label><br>
        <textarea name="allergy" rows="4" cols="57">
        </textarea>
    </div><br>
    <div>
        <label for="medications">Please list any medications you are
          currently taking</label><br>
        <textarea name= "medications" rows="4" cols="57">
        </textarea>
    </div><br>
    <div>
        <label for="pregnancy">If you are a woman, are you currently
          pregnant, or is there a possibility that you are pregnant?
          </label><br>
        <input type="radio" name="pregnancy"><label>Yes</label>
        <input type="radio" name="pregnancy"><label>No</label>
        <input type="radio" name="pregnancy"><label>Not Applicable
          </label>
    </div><br>
    <div>
        <label for="healthrating">In general, would you say your
          health is</label><br>
        * Taking 1 to be poor and 5 to be excellent<br>
        <input type="number" name="healthrating" min="1" max="5">
    </div><br>
        <label for="ratinghealth">When you think about your health
          care, how much do you agree or disagree with this statement:
          "I receive exactly what I want and need exactly when and how
          I want and need it."</label><br>
        * Taking 1 to be strongly dis-agree and 5 to be strongly
          agree<br>
        1<input type="range" name="ratinghealth" min="1" max="5">5
    </div>
</fieldset>

<div class="submit">
  <input type="submit" value="Submit">
</div>
```

The output of the code is as follows:

Medical Information
Check all that apply to you or your immediate family?
☐ Asthma
☐ Cancer
☐ HIV and AIDS
☐ Diabetes
☐ Hypertension
☐ Malaria
☐ Seizure Disorder
☐ Psychiatric Disorders
☐ Mental Health
☐ Stroke
☐ Others
☐ Not Applicable

Check all symptoms you are currently experiencing
☐ Allergy
☐ Eye
☐ Lymphatic
☐ Fever
☐ Eating Disorder
☐ Hemtalogical
☐ Musculoskeletal Pain
☐ Skin
☐ Gastrointestinal
☐ Weight Loss
☐ Others
☐ Not Applicable

Please list any medication allergies that you have

Please list any medications you are currently taking

If you are a woman, are you currently pregnant, or is there a possibility that you are pregnant?
○ Yes ○ No ○ Not Applicable

In general, would you say your health is
* Taking 1 to be poor and 5 to be excellent

When you think about your health care, how much do you agree or disagree with this statement: "I receive exactly what I want and need exactly when and how I want and need it."
* Taking 1 to be strongly dis-agree and 5 to be strongly agree
1 ——————————————— 5

Submit

Our final section of the form asks the respondents about their medical information. To get information about various diseases or symptoms a respondent has, we have used the basic HTML `<form>` `<input>` type `checkbox`.

`Textarea` is a free text field, which contains detailed text and, in our case, allows the respondent to enter information, such as medication allergies and medication. The rows and columns of the `textarea` determine the displayable size of the `textarea` text field in the form. We can also set the limit by setting `maxlength` to restrict the respondent from entering lengthy details.

`radiobutton` is used to restrict the respondent from choosing only one option from multiple options.

With the `<input>` type `number`, we created a spinner, which is a precise control for selecting the string represented by a number. Here, we have set the limit by setting the min value to `1` and the max value to `5`.

With the `<input>` type `range`, we created a slider, which is an imprecise control for setting the value to a string representing a number. Here, we have set the limit by setting the min value to `1` and the max value to `5`.

Finally, the `<input>` type `submit` sends the data to the server.

Guidelines

A good practice or guideline is to design and develop a standard approach, which has always shown better results.

Some of the best practices to create effective forms are as follows:

- Use relevant content groupings to organize forms
- Minimize the amount of help and tips required to fill out a form
- Employ flexible data entry
- For long forms, show progress and save options
- Maintain a consistent approach
- Maintain a clear relationship between the initial selection options
- Use inline validation of inputs that have potentially high error rates
- Provide actionable remedies to correct errors
- Disable the **Submit** button after a user clicks on it to avoid multiple submissions
- Clearly communicate about the submission of data and provide feedback
- Maintain separate files for CSS and JavaScript

Using best practices:

- Improves cross-browser compatibility
- Increases performance
- Saves time and reduces cost
- Project understanding becomes easy
- Code maintenance becomes easy

Summary

In this chapter, we learned about forms and the benefits of using them. We have seen the difference between basic HTML forms and HTML5 forms.

We learned about the new `<form>` controls, `date`, `week`, `tel`, `email`, `range`, `numbers`, and many more for which we do not have to rely on JavaScript and how they work in the modern browsers.

We also built a sample form to get well versed with the forms and at the end of the chapter we learned the best practices to create effective web forms.

Overall, we've seen ways to reduce the amount of scripting and development time when users need to create full-featured forms with the help of HTML5.

2
Validation of Forms

Form validation has always been tricky and painful for developers since the Web was born. Before HTML5, it was a nightmare for developers to write lines of code for validating forms to get the desired information from the user.

In this chapter, we will cover the following topics:

- Validation, their benefits, and their types
- HTML5 `<input>` and attributes used in validations
- The difference between JavaScript and HTML5 validations with an example
- Validation constraints and supported APIs (Application Programming interface)
- Default error messages displayed by the browser

Form validation

Validation of a form is a series of checks and notifications that guides a user as to what is required as an input while submitting information to a server. We can also say that it is a process of checking the input data against a specific standard or requirement.

Form validation is a process for detecting invalid control data and displaying those errors to the end users. The term has several benefits as follows:

- Provides the necessary instructions and hints
- Provides a logical reading and navigation order of the elements
- Users can easily get to know the mistakes they have made while entering the data

- Ensures that the form can be completed and submitted using the keyboard
- Saves users' waiting time on an HTTP request or a network call
- Saves the owner's server time and memory from dealing with bad inputs

Validation ensures that sufficient data has been provided by the user, such as with online shopping, which typically includes the address, e-mail address, and many more details which are mandatory for a transaction to be complete.

There are many methods to perform form validations, which can be categorized into the following:

- Client-side form validation
- Server-side form validation

Client-side form validation

Client-side validation can be performed using HTML5 attributes on a browser that supports them or even with the help of JavaScript for other browsers. HTML5 attributes reduce the effort of validation in comparison to cumbersome JavaScript validations.

The advantages of client-side form validation are as follows:

- It enhances the experience of the user by responding quickly at the client side itself
- Validation can occur as the `<form>` controls are filled by the user before submitting the form to the server
- This approach is quite simple as it ensures that the user has filled the required fields with valid data and also guides the user while filling up the form correctly
- It's a fast form of validation as it does not require any server-side scripting

The disadvantages of client-side form validation are as follows:

- It can be disabled in the client's browser and does not provide any security mechanism
- This approach cannot protect our application from various security concerns while transmitting the data along the network
- Client-side validation provides minimum security as it can be altered or bypassed very easily

Server-side form validation

Various scripting languages, such as PHP, ASP, or Perl are used to screen and filter the data submitted by the user at server side.

This approach is used when we know that some checks can be performed only on the server side as security is required, as in the case of online shopping, where the user enters card details for making a payment.

The advantages of server-side form validation are as follows:

- The valid and complete information can be submitted without any error recovery messages and warnings.

- Every page that a user sees in the browser is downloaded to the computer, which includes JavaScript that has validation code. So, a hacker can create a new version of the page without any validation and can fool our server by entering invalid data. In such scenarios, server-side validations are helpful.

- Server-side validation is more secure and cannot be altered or bypassed easily.

The disadvantages of server-side form validation are as follows:

- This approach requires more response time leading to poor user experience

- The server-side processing code resubmits the page so as to display the error messages

- To have the minimum number of request-response life cycles, it validates all form fields at the same time

More or less, we all have relied on JavaScript to validate forms. Also, we should always keep in mind that client-side form validation is not a replacement for foolproof server-side validation and handling errors. It is an efficient means of providing an instant feedback on the input of the user at the client end. In case of online shopping, the user selects total number of pieces, but after a certain limit, the user sees an error that the limit has been exceeded. All these validations demand high-end server-side validations, which is not possible on the client side. Always remember, in case of forms, use server-side validations.

HTML5 form validation

The purpose of introducing HTML5 validation is to notify a user that a page contains some mandatory information that needs to be filled or corrects the users for any errors using the browser's built-in processing. We should take advantage of all the capabilities and knowledge that the browser has, to catch errors within a form, before sending it to the server. Also, we need not bother about the time and expense of a network round-trip or getting a response from the server about some stupid error.

New <input> attributes such as required and pattern used in combination with CSS pseudo-class selectors make it easier to write the checks and display feedback to the user. There are also other advanced validation techniques that allow you to use JavaScript to set custom validity rules and messages or to determine whether an element is invalid and why.

Before we go deeper into HTML5 validations, let us see the difference when the client-side validation is performed using JavaScript and how we can validate using HTML5 <form> controls. Here, in the following instance, we are validating a simple textbox which is mandatory to be filled in by the user.

Code 1 – validating a textbox using JavaScript

The following code will validate a textbox using JavaScript:

```
<head>
<script>
  function validateField()
  {
    var x=document.forms["Field"]["fname"].value;
    if (x==null || x==""){
      alert("Please enter your name");
      return false;
    }
  }
</script>
</head>
<body>
  <form name="Field" action="#" onsubmit="validateField()"
    method= "post">
  First name: <input type= "text" name= "fname">
  <input type= "submit" value= "Submit">
</form>
</body>
```

The output of the preceding code will be as shown in the following screenshot:

Code 2 – validating a textbox using HTML5 <form> controls

The following code will validate a textbox using HTML5:

```
<head>
<script>
</script>
</head>
<body>
  <form name= "Field" action= "#">
  First name: <input type= "text" name= "fname" required>
  <input type= "submit" value= "Submit">
</form>
</body>
```

The output of the preceding code will be as shown in the following screenshot:

In the preceding two code examples, we saw how the `<script>` part in the first code was replaced by a single attribute of the HTML5 `<form>` control in the second code, which not only reduced the lines of code, but also removed the scope of JavaScript.

Constraint validations

The algorithm that browsers run to determine the validity of a form when it is submitted is called constraint validation. To constrain data or check validity, the algorithm utilizes new HTML5 attributes such as `min`, `max`, `step`, `pattern`, and `required`, as well as existing attributes such as `maxlength` and `type`.

In HTML5, basic constraints are declared in two different ways:

- By choosing the most semantically appropriate value for the `type` attribute of the `<input>` element
- By setting values on validation-related attributes and allowing basic constraints to be described in a simple way without the need for JavaScript

HTML5 constraint validation APIs

Nowadays, an increasing number of browsers are supporting the constraint validation API, and it's becoming more and more reliable. However, HTML5 constraint validation doesn't remove the need for validation on the server side.

At a high level, this API covers the following features:

- Form fields have a validity property
- Form fields also have a generic `checkValidity()` method
- Finally, there is a `setCustomValidity()` method

The validity object

The `validity` object is a set of keys and Boolean values that represent the validity of a particular form. In simple terms, we can say that it tells what a particular form lacks.

Let us take the numeric field type as an example to understand this. With the numeric field type, we can specify that a form field should be numeric and we can set the limitation; for example, the number should be higher than 0 and less than 25. The `validity` property would actually be able to tell you if the value wasn't a number or was too low or too high.

The `validity` object of a DOM node returns a `ValidityState` object containing a number of Boolean properties related to the validity of the data in the node. In a `ValidityState` object, whenever we get a reference to it, we can keep a hold of it, and the validity checks that we get in return will update as needed when the changes occur as shown in the following code example:

```
<head>
<script>
  function validateInput(){
    var bool1=
      document.getElementById('handbook1').validity.customError;
    var result1=document.getElementById('result1').
      innerHTML = bool1;
  }
</script>
</head>
<body>
  <input type= "text" id="handbook1">
  <div>
  <label>Result1:</label><output id="result1" ></output>
  </div>
  <input type="button" value="Validate" onclick="validateInput()">
</body>
```

The checkValidity method

The `checkValidity` method is called to check for the value that this method returns for the successful and unsuccessful validation scenarios. It returns a Boolean value, and we can use this method when there is no need to know why a field is invalid, or we can use this method before we sneak into the `validity` property to know why the field is not valid.

This method allows us to check validation on the form without any input from the user.

Validation of form is checked whenever the user or the script code submits the form, but this method allows validation to be done at any time, as shown in the following code example:

```
<head>
<script>
  function validateInput(){
    //false
    var bool2=document.getElementById('handbook2')
      .checkValidity(); //true
```

```
        var result1=document.getElementById('result1').
          innerHTML = bool1;
        var result2=document.getElementById('result2').
          innerHTML = bool2;
    }
  </script>
  </head>
  <body>
    <input type= "text" id="handbook1" required>
    <input type= "text" id="handbook2" value="handbook">
    <div>
    <label>Result1:</label><output id="result1"></output>
    </div>
    <div>
    <label>Result2:</label><output id="result2"></output>
    </div>
    <input type="button" value="Validate" onclick="validateInput()">
  </body>
```

The output of the preceding code will be as shown in the following screenshot:

The setCustomValidity() method

The setCustomValidity() method lets us decide logically and create a custom validation error message and display it when an invalid input is submitted to the form. This lets us use JavaScript code to establish a validation failure other than those offered by the standard constraint validation APIs. The message is displayed while reporting the problem.

This method also allows us to set a message and sets the field as being in an error state by default. If the argument is the empty string, the custom error is cleared or is considered valid. When we do not customize the error message using the setCustomValidity() method, the built-in error message is displayed, as shown in the following code example:

```
<script>
  function check(input){
    if (input.value !=
      document.getElementById('email_addr').value) {
      input.setCustomValidity('Both the email addresses must
        match.');
    }
    else{
      input.setCustomValidity('');
    }
  }
</script>
<body>
  <form id="myForm">
  <div>
  <label>Enter Email Address:</label>
  <input type="email" id="email_addr" name="email_addr">
  </div>
  <div>
  <label>Repeat Email Address:</label>
  <input type="email" id="email_addr_repeat"
    name="email_addr_repeat">
  </div>
  <input type="submit" value="Validate" onclick="check(this)">
</form>
```

The output of the preceding code will be as shown in the following screenshot:

The willValidate attribute

The willValidate attribute indicates whether an element will be validated based on the form's validation rules and constraints. If any of the constraints, such as the required attribute or the pattern attribute, are set on the control, the willValidate field will let you know that validation checking will be enforced.

This attribute returns **true** if the element will be validated when the form is submitted; otherwise, it will return **false,** as shown in the following code example:

```
<script>
  function validateInput(){
    var bool1= document.getElementById('handbook1').
      willValidate; //true
    var bool2=document.getElementById('handbook2').
      willValidate; //undefined
    var bool3= document.getElementById('handbook3').
      willValidate; //false
    var result1=document.getElementById('result1').
      innerHTML = bool1;
    var result2=document.getElementById('result2').
      innerHTML = bool2;
    var result3=document.getElementById('result3').
      innerHTML = bool3;
  }
</script>
<body>
  <input type= "text" id="handbook1" required value= "handbook">
  <div id= "handbook2" type="text">
  <input type= "text" id="handbook3" disabled>
  <div>
  <label>Result1:</label><output id="result1" ></output>
  </div>
  <div>
  <label>Result2:</label><output id="result2" ></output>
  </div>
  <div>
  <label>Result3:</label><output id="result3" ></output>
  </div>
  <input type="button" value="Validate" onclick="validateInput()">
</body>
```

The output of the preceding code will be as shown in the following screenshot:

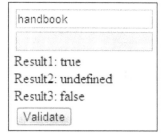

The validationMessage attribute

The validationMessage attribute allows us to programmatically query a localized error message that the control does not satisfy. If the control is not a candidate for constraint validation, or if the element's value satisfies its constraints, validationMessage sets to an empty string.

For instance, if a required field has no input, the browser will present its default error message to the user. Once supported, this is the text string that will be returned by the validationMessage field as shown in the following code example:

```
<script>
  function validateInput(){
    var bool1=
      document.getElementById('handbook1').validationMessage;
    var bool2=document.getElementById('handbook2').
      validationMessage;
    var result1=document.getElementById('result1').
      innerHTML = bool1;
    var result2=document.getElementById('result2').
      innerHTML = bool2;
  }
</script>
<body>
  <input type= "text" id="handbook1" required/>
  <input type= "text" id="handbook2" value= "handbook">
  <div>
  <label>Result1:</label><output id="result1" ></output>
  </div>
  <div>
  <label>Result2:</label><output id="result2" ></output>
  </div>
```

```
<input type="button" value="Validate" onclick="validateInput()">
</body>
```

The output of the preceding code will look as shown in the following screenshot:

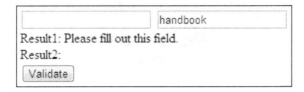

HTML5 provides us with several ways to enforce correctness on forms; that is, HTML5 provides several validity constraints on any given <form> control.

As mentioned previously, several validity constraints on any given <form> control are discussed in this section.

The patternMismatch property

The patternMismatch property is used to set any pattern rule on a <form> control and returns if the <input> value matches the rules defined by the pattern attribute.

The validity.patternMismatch attribute

- If the element's value does not match the provided pattern attribute, it returns **true**; otherwise, it returns **false**

- The element will match the :invalid CSS pseudo-class when it returns **true** as shown in the following code example:

```
<script>
  function validateInput(){
    var bool1= document.getElementById('handbook1').
      validity.patternMismatch; //false
    var bool2= document.getElementById('handbook2').
      validity.patternMismatch; //true
    var result1=document.getElementById('result1').
      innerHTML = bool1;
    var result2=document.getElementById('result2').
      innerHTML = bool2;
  }
</script>
<body>
  <input type= "text" id="handbook1" pattern="[0-9]{5}"
    value="123456">
```

```
<input type= "text" id="handbook2" pattern="[a-z]{3}"
  value="xyz">
<div>
<label>Result1:</label>  <output id="result1"></output>
</div>
<div>
<label>Result2:</label>  <output id="result2"></output>
</div>
<input type="button" value="Validate"
  onclick="validateInput()">
</body>
```

The output of the preceding code will be as shown in the following screenshot:

The customError property

The customError property is used to handle the errors that are calculated and set by the application code. This property validates whether the customized error message is set or not.

It is used to call the setCustomValidity() property to put a form control into the customError state.

The validity.customError property

If the element has a custom error, it returns **true**; otherwise, it returns **false,** as shown in the following code example:

```
<script>
  function validateInput(){
    Var bool1=document.getElementById('handbook1').
      validity.customError; //false
    var bool2= document.getElementById('handbook2').
      setCustomValidity('Invalid Message');
    var bool3= document.getElementById('handbook2').
      validity.customError; //true
    var result1=document.getElementById('result1').
      innerHTML = bool1;
```

```
      var result2=document.getElementById('result2').
        innerHTML = bool2;
      var result3=document.getElementById('result3').
        innerHTML = bool3;
  }
</script>
<body>
  <input type= "text" id="handbook1">
  <input type= "text" id="handbook2">
  <div>
  <label>Result1:</label>  <output id="result1" ></output>
  </div>
  <div>
  <label>Result2:</label>  <output id="result2" ></output>
  </div>
  <div>
  <label>Result3:</label>  <output id="result3" ></output>
  </div>
  <input type="button" value="Validate" onclick="validateInput()">
</body>
```

The output of the preceding code will be as shown in the following screenshot:

The rangeOverflow property

The rangeOverflow property is used to notify that the input value of the <form> control is greater than the maximum value or that the input value is out of range.

This property checks the max attribute to a <form> control with the maximum input value.

The validity.rangeOverflow property

- If the element's value is higher than the provided maximum value, it returns **true**; otherwise, it returns **false**

- The element will match the :invalid and :out-of-range CSS pseudo-classes when it returns **true**, as shown in the following code example:

```
<script>
  function validateInput(){
    var bool1= document.getElementById('handbook1').
      validity.rangeOverflow; //false
    var bool2=document.getElementById('handbook2').
      validity.rangeOverflow; //true
    var result1=document.getElementById('result1').
      innerHTML = bool1;
    var result2=document.getElementById('result2').
      innerHTML = bool2;
  }
</script>
<body>
  <input type= "number" id="handbook1" max="3" value="1">
  <input type= "number" id="handbook2" max="3" value="4">
  <div>
  <label>Result1:</label>  <output id="result1" ></output>
  </div>
  <div>
  <label>Result2:</label>  <output id="result2" ></output>
  </div>
  <input type="button" value="Validate"
    onclick="validateInput()">
</body>
```

The output of the preceding code will be as shown inthe following screenshot:

The rangeUnderflow property

The rangeUnderflow property is used to notify that the input value of the <form> control is lower than the minimum value.

This property checks the min attribute to a <form> control with the minimum input value.

The validity.rangeUnderflow property

- If the element's value is lower than the provided minimum value, it returns **true;** otherwise, it returns **false**

- The element will match the :invalid and :out-of-range CSS pseudo-classes when it returns **true,** as shown in the following code example:

```
<script>
  function validateInput(){
    var bool1= document.getElementById('handbook1').
      validity.rangeUnderflow; //true
    var bool2= document.getElementById('handbook2').
      validity.rangeUnderflow; //false
    var result1=document.getElementById('result1').
      innerHTML = bool1;
    var result2=document.getElementById('result2').
      innerHTML = bool2;
  }
</script>
<body>
  <input type= "number" id="handbook1" min="3" value="1">
  <input type= "number" id="handbook2" min="3" value="4">
  <div>
  <label>Result1:</label>  <output id="result1" ></output>
  </div>
  <div>
  <label>Result2:</label>  <output id="result2" ></output>
  </div>
  <input type="button" value="Validate"
    onclick="validateInput()">
</body>
```

The output of the preceding code will look as shown in the following screenshot:

The stepMismatch property

The `stepMismatch` property ensures that an `<input>` value complies with the rules or standards of the values of `min`, `max`, and `step`. For example, if the step value is five and the value entered is three, we will have a step mismatch in this case.

The validity.stepMismatch property

- If the element's value doesn't fit the rules given by the `step` attribute, it returns **true**; otherwise, it returns **false**

- The element will match the `:invalid` and `:out-of-range` CSS pseudo-classes when it returns **true,** as shown in the following code example:

```
<script>
  function validateInput(){
    var bool1= document.getElementById('handbook1').
      validity.stepMismatch; //true
    var bool2= document.getElementById('handbook2').
      validity.stepMismatch; //false
    var result1=document.getElementById('result1').
      innerHTML = bool1;
    var result2=document.getElementById('result2').
      innerHTML = bool2;
  }
</script>
<body>
  <input type= "number" id="handbook1" step="3" value="1">
  <input type= "number" id="handbook2" step="3" value="6">
  <div>
  <label>Result1:</label>  <output id="result1" ></output>
  </div>
  <div>
  <label>Result2:</label>  <output id="result2" ></output>
  </div>
  <input type="button" value="Validate"
    onclick="validateInput()">
</body>
```

The output of the preceding code will be as shown in the following screenshot:

The tooLong property

This property ensures that an `<input>` field does not contain too many characters.

We ensure this by adding a `maxlength` attribute on the `<form>` control.

The validity.tooLong property

- If the element's value is longer than the provided maximum length, it returns **true;** otherwise, it returns **false**

- The element will match the `:invalid` and `:out-of-range` CSS pseudo-classes when it returns **true,** as shown in the following code example:

```
<script>
  function validateInput(){
    var bool1=   document.getElementById('handbook1').
      validity.tooLong; //false
    var bool2=     document.getElementById('handbook2').
      validity.tooLong; //true
    var result1=document.getElementById('result1').
      innerHTML = bool1;
    var result2=document.getElementById('result2').
      innerHTML = bool2;
    }
</script>
<body>
  <input type="text" id="handbook1" maxlength="5"
    value="12345678"/>
  <input type="text" id="handbook2" maxlength="5"
    value="xyz"/>
  <div>
  <label>Result1:</label>  <output id="result1" ></output>
  </div>
  <div>
  <label>Result2:</label>  <output id="result2" ></output>
  </div>
```

```
<input type="button" value="Validate"
  onclick="validateInput()">
</body>
```

The output of the preceding code will be as shown in the following screenshot:

The typeMismatch property

The `typeMismatch` property is used to notify that the `<input>` value does not match with the `<form>` control in cases such as e-mail, URL, and number, and ensures that the type of value matches its expected field.

The validity.typeMismatch property

- If the element's value is not in the correct syntax, it returns **true**; otherwise, it returns **false**

- The element will match the `:invalid` CSS pseudo-class when it returns **true**, as shown in the following code example:

```
<script>
  function validateInput(){
    var bool1= document.getElementById('handbook1').
      validity.typeMismatch; //false
    var bool2= document.getElementById('handbook2').
      validity.typeMismatch; //true
    var result1=document.getElementById('result1').
      innerHTML = bool1;
    var result2=document.getElementById('result2').
      innerHTML = bool2;
  }
</script>
<body>
  <input type="email" id="handbook1"
    value="handbook@books.com">
  <input type="email" id="handbook2" value="handbook">
  <div>
  <label>Result1:</label>  <output id="result1" ></output>
  </div>
```

```
      <div>
      <label>Result2:</label>  <output id="result2" ></output>
      </div>
      <input type="button" value="Validate"
        onclick="validateInput()">
  </body>
```

The output of the preceding code will be as shown in the following screenshot:

The valueMissing property

The `valueMissing` property ensures that some value is set on the `<form>` control. To ensure this, set the required attribute on the `<form>` control to **true**.

The validity.valueMissing property

- If the element has no value but is a required field, it returns **true**; otherwise, it returns **false**

- The element will match the `:invalid` CSS pseudo-class when it returns **true**, as shown in the following code example:

```
<script>
  function validateInput(){
    var bool1=document.getElementById('handbook1').
      validity.valueMissing; //false
    var bool2= document.getElementById('handbook2').
      validity.valueMissing; //true
    var result1=document.getElementById('result1').
      innerHTML = bool1;
    var result2=document.getElementById('result2').
      innerHTML = bool2;
  }
</script>
<body>
  <input type= "text" id="handbook1" required
    value="handbook">
  <input type= "text" id="handbook2" required value="">
  <div>
```

```
   <label>Result1:</label>  <output id="result1" ></output>
   </div>
   <div>
   <label>Result2:</label>  <output id="result2" ></output>
   </div>
   <input type="button" value="Validate"
     onclick="validateInput()">
 </body>
```

The output of the preceding code will look as shown in the following screenshot:

The valid property

The valid property is used to check whether the field is valid.

The validity.valid property

*   If the element's value has no validity problems, it returns **true**; otherwise, it returns **false**

*   The element will match the :invalid CSS pseudo-class when it returns **true,** as shown in the following code example:

```
<script>
  function validateInput(){
    var bool1= document.getElementById('handbook1').
      validity.valid; //true
    var bool2= document.getElementById('handbook2').
      validity.valid; //false
    var result1=document.getElementById('result1').
      innerHTML = bool1;
    var result2=document.getElementById('result2').
      innerHTML = bool2;;
  }
</script>
<body>
  <input type= "text" id="handbook1" required
    value="handbook">
```

```
<input type= "text" id="handbook2" required value="">
<div>
<label>Result1:</label>  <output id="result1" ></output>
</div>
<div>
<label>Result2:</label>  <output id="result2" ></output>
</div>
<input type="button" value="Validate"
  onclick="validateInput()">
</body>
```

The output of the preceding code will be as shown in the following screenshot:

The following table shows the various attributes with their possible values and associated violations:

Attribute	<Input> types supporting the attribute	Possible values	Constraint description	Associated violation
required	date, month, week, checkbox, radio button, URL, telephone, e-mail, text, password, search, time, range, number and tags such as <select>, <textarea>, checkbox, and radiobutton	It returns the Boolean value None; when present, it returns **true** and when absent, it returns **false**	The value is to be filled mandatorily	Constraint violation: Missing

Attribute	\<Input\> types supporting the attribute	Possible values	Constraint description	Associated violation
min	number and range	Must be a valid number	The filled parameter must be greater than or equal to the value defined	Constraint violation: Underflow
	month, date, and week	Must be a valid date		
	datetime-local, time, and datetime	Must be a valid date and time		
maxlength	tags such as \<textarea\> and attributes are text, password, search, tel, url, and email	Must be an integer length	The value of the attribute must not be greater than the number of characters filled	Constraint violation: Too long
max	number and range	Must be a valid number	The filled parameter must be lesser than or equal to the value defined	Constraint violation: Overflow
	month ,date, and week	Must be a valid date		
	datetime-local, time, and datetime	Must be a valid date and time		
pattern	text, search, URL, telephone, e-mail, and password	It is a regular expression defined using JavaScript	The value of the attribute must exactly match the pattern defined	Constraint violation: Pattern mismatch
step	month	Must be an integer number of months	Until the value of step is set to the any literal (values available in the step menu), value will be min value plus an integral multiple of step	Constraint violation: Step mismatch
	date	Must be an integer number of days		
	week	Must be an integer number of weeks		
	datetime, datetime-local, and time	Must be an integer number of seconds		
	number and range	Must be an integer		

Error messages

Nowadays, all modern browsers support most of the features of HTML5. The functionality of the features is the same in all browsers but there are some differences; one of which is the default error message that the browser, displays.

Some of the default error messages displayed by various browsers are shown in the following screenshot:

However, we can change the default error message of the browser with the help of setCustomvalidity. Let us understand this with an example.

The following code changes the default error message of a browser to a custom message:

```
<script>
  function check()
  {
    varhtmlObject=document.getElementById("input");
    if (!htmlObject.checkValidity()) {
      htmlObject.setCustomValidity('This field is mandatory');
    }
  }
</script>
<body>
```

```
      <form id="myForm">
      <input id="input" type="text" required />
      <input type="submit" onclick="check(this)">
      </form>
   </body>
```

The preceding code will give the following output:

Summary

In this chapter, we learned about form validation and their types. We also learned the benefits of the different types of validations. We have also seen the various <input> types and attributes used in the validation of forms.

We have seen the difference between JavaScript validation and HTML5 validation by building a sample code.

Next, we learned about constraint validations and the various APIs supported by HTML5.

Lastly, we saw the various browser-specific default error messages and learned how to change the browser's default error message.

3
Styling the Forms

In earlier chapters, we learned how to build a form using HTML5, but CSS3 is used by web designers and developers to give web forms a rich and elegant look. With the basic understanding of CSS3, in this chapter we will learn how to improve the look and feel of the forms.

In this chapter, we will cover the following topics:

- CSS3 and its modules
- Styling the forms
- Guidelines for effective styling of the forms

CSS3 for web forms

CSS3 brings us infinite new possibilities and allows styling to make better web forms. CSS3 gives us a number of new ways to create an impact with our form designs, with quite a few important changes. HTML5 introduced useful new form elements such as sliders and spinners and old elements such as `textbox` and `textarea`, and we can make them look really cool with our innovation and CSS3. Using CSS3, we can turn an old and boring form into a modern, cool, and eye catching one.

CSS3 is completely backwards compatible, so we will not have to change the existing form designs. Browsers have and will always support CSS2.

CSS3 forms can be split up into modules. Some of the most important CSS3 modules are:

- Selectors (with pseudo-selectors)
- Backgrounds and Borders
- Text (with Text Effects)

- Fonts
- Gradients

Styling of forms always varies with requirements and the innovation of the web designer or developer. In this chapter, we will look at those CSS3 properties with which we can style our forms and give them a rich and elegant look.

Some of the new properties of CSS3 required vendor prefixes, which were used frequently as they helped browsers to read the code. In general, it is no longer needed to use them with CSS3 for some of the properties, such as `border-radius`, but they come into action when the browser doesn't interpret the code. A list of all the vendor prefixes for major browsers is given as follows:

- `-moz-`: Firefox
- `-webkit-`: WebKit browsers such as Safari and Chrome
- `-o-`: Opera
- `-ms-`: Internet Explorer

Before we start styling the form, let us have a quick revision of form modules for better understanding and styling of the forms.

Selectors and pseudo-selectors

Selectors are a pattern used to select the elements which we want to style. A selector can contain one or more simple selectors separated by combinators. The CSS3 Selectors module introduces three new attribute selectors; they are grouped together under the heading **Substring Matching Attribute Selectors**.

These new selectors are as follows:

- `[att^=val]`: The "begins with" selector
- `[att$=val]`: The "ends with" selector
- `[att*=val]`: The "contains" selector

The first of these new selectors, which we will refer to as the "begins with" selector, allows the selection of elements where a specified attribute (for example, the `href` attribute of a hyperlink) begins with a specified string (for example, `http://`, `https://`, or `mailto:`).

In the same way, the additional two new selectors, which we will refer to as the "ends with" and "contains" selectors, allow the selection of elements where a specified attribute either ends with or contains a specified string respectively.

A CSS pseudo-class is just an additional keyword to selectors that tells a special state of the element to be selected. For example, `:hover` will apply a style when the user hovers over the element specified by the selector. Pseudo-classes, along with pseudo-elements, apply a style to an element not only in relation to the content of the document tree, but also in relation to external factors like the history of the navigator, such as `:visited`, and the status of its content, such as `:checked`, on some form elements.

The new pseudo-classes are as follows:

Type	Details
`:last-child`	It is used to match an element that is the last child element of its parent element.
`:first-child`	It is used to match an element that is the first child element of its parent element.
`:checked`	It is used to match elements such as radio buttons or checkboxes which are checked.
`:first-of-type`	It is used to match the first child element of the specified element type.
`:last-of-type`	It is used to match the last child element of the specified element type.
`:nth-last-of-type(N)`	It is used to match the Nth child element from the last of the specified element type.
`:only-child`	It is used to match an element if it's the only child element of its parent.
`:only-of-type`	It is used to match an element that is the only child element of its type.
`:root`	It is used to match the element that is the root element of the document.
`:empty`	It is used to match elements that have no children.
`:target`	It is used to match the current active element that is the target of an identifier in the document's URL.
`:enabled`	It is used to match user interface elements that are enabled.
`:nth-child(N)`	It is used to match every Nth child element of the parent.
`:nth-of-type(N)`	It is used to match every Nth child element of the parent counting from the last of the parent .
`:disabled`	It is used to match user interface elements that are disabled.

Type	Details
:not(S)	It is used to match elements that aren't matched by the specified selector.
:nth-last-child(N)	Within a parent element's list of child elements, it is used to match elements on the basis of their positions.

Backgrounds

CSS3 contains several new background attributes; and moreover, in CSS3, some changes are also made in the previous properties of the background; which allow greater control on the background element.

The new background properties added are as follows.

The background-clip property

The background-clip property is used to determine the allowable area for the background image.

If there is no background image, then this property has only visual effects such as when the border has transparent regions or partially opaque regions; otherwise, the border covers up the difference.

Syntax

The syntax for the background-clip property are as follows:

```
background-clip: no-clip / border-box / padding-box / content-box;
```

Values

The values for the background-clip property is as follows:

- border-box: With this, the background extends to the outside edge of the border
- padding-box: With this, no background is drawn below the border
- content-box: With this, the background is painted within the content box; only the area the content covers is painted
- no-clip: This is the default value, same as border-box

The background-origin property

The `background-origin` property specifies the positioning of the background image or color with respect to the `background-position` property.

This property has no effect if the `background-attachment` property for the background image is fixed.

Syntax

The following is the syntax for the `background-attachment` property:

```
background-origin: border-box / padding-box / content-box;
```

Values

The values for the `background-attachment` property are as follows:

- `border-box`: With this, the background extends to the outside edge of the border
- `padding-box`: By using this, no background is drawn below the border
- `content-box`: With this, the background is painted within the content box

The background-size property

The `background-size` property specifies the size of the background image.

If this property is not specified then the original size of the image will be displayed.

Syntax

The following is the syntax for the `background-size` property:

```
background-size: length / percentage / cover / contain;
```

Values

The values for the `background-size` property are as follows:

- `length`: This specifies the height and width of the background image. No negative values are allowed.
- `percentage`: This specifies the height and width of the background image in terms of the percent of the parent element.

- `cover`: This specifies the background image to be as large as possible so that the background area is completely covered.
- `contain`: This specifies the image to the largest size such that its width and height can fit inside the content area.

Apart from adding new properties, CSS3 has also enhanced some old background properties, which are as follows.

The background-color property

If the underlying layer of the background image of the element cannot be used, we can specify a fallback color in addition to specifying a background color.

We can implement this by adding a forward slash before the fallback color.

```
background-color: red / blue;
```

The background-repeat property

In CSS2 when an image is repeated at the end, the image often gets cut off. CSS3 introduced new properties with which we can fix this problem:

- `space`: By using this property between the image tiles, an equal amount of space is applied until they fill the element
- `round`: By using this property until the tiles fit the element, the image is scaled down

The background-attachment property

With the new possible value of `local`, we can now set the background to scroll when the element's content is scrolled.

This comes into action with elements that can scroll. For example:

```
body{background-image:url('example.gif');background-repeat:no-
    repeat;background-attachment:fixed;}
```

CSS3 allows web designers and developers to have multiple background images, using nothing but just a simple comma-separated list. For example:

```
background-image: url(abc.png), url(xyz.png);
```

Borders

The `border` property allows us to specify the style and color of an element's border, and with the help of CSS3 we have stepped into the next level.

With CSS3, we can create rounded borders, add shadow, and use an image as a border without using various design programs such as Photoshop.

The new border properties added are as follows.

The border-radius property

Creating rounded borders using CSS was never easy. There were numerous methods available, but none of the approaches were straightforward. Moreover, it was necessary to use vendor prefixes for both WebKit and Mozilla, in order to apply the style correctly.

The `border-radius` property can be applied to customize buttons. We can also apply `border-radius` to individual corners. And with the help of this property, we can create rounded borders easily.

Syntax

The syntax for the `border-radius` property is given as follows:

```
border-radius: 1-4 length / % ;
```

Values

Following are the values of the `border-radius` property:

- `length`: This defines the size of the radius of the circle
- `%`: This defines the size of the radius of the circle using percentage values

The box-shadow property

The `box-shadow` property allows designers and developers to create multiple drop shadows easily. These can be outside or inside the boxes, specifying values for color, size, blur, and offset.

By simply declaring `box-shadow` once, we can use both `outer` and `inset` versions, separated by a comma.

Syntax

The syntax for the box-shadow property is as follows:

```
box-shadow: h-shadow v-shadow blur spread color inset;
```

Values

The following shows the values of the box-shadow property:

- inset: This changes the outer (outset) shadow to the inner shadow
- <h-shadow>, <v-shadow>: This specifies the position of the shadow
- <blur>: The larger this value, the bigger the blur
- <spread>: This specifies the size of the shadow
- <color>: This specifies the color of the shadow

The border-image property

The border-image property is a little tricky, but it allows us to create boxes with custom borders. With this feature, you can define an image to be used as a border instead of the normal border.

We can create decorative borders beyond simple rounded corners with images or even with gradients.

This feature is actually split into a couple of properties:

- border-image
- border-corner-image

Syntax

The syntax for the border-image property are as follows:

```
border-image: <source><slice><width><outset><repeat>;
```

Values

The values of the border-image property is given as:

- source: This specifies the image to be used for the border.
- slice: This specifies the inward offsets of the border.
- width: This specifies the width of the border.

- `outset`: This specifies how much the border image area extends beyond the border box.

- `repeat`: This specifies whether the border should be stretched or not. If yes, then whether it is rounded or stretched.

Text effects

We have seen many websites with various text effects, and they are rapidly getting popular as the current and upcoming trend for good form design. With the help of CSS3, the best thing about these effects is that they can be achieved with pure CSS, that is, no more image replacements and image-heavy design. In this section, we will learn some new text effects that CSS3 provides us.

The new text features are as follows.

The text-shadow property

The `text-shadow` property is used to apply shadow effects to the text content. We can have one or more effects for a single text by using a simple comma.

These effects consist of a shadow color, x/y offset of the shadow effect, and a blurring radius for the shadow effect. The effects can overlap each other, but for clarity they should not overlap the text content.

Syntax

The syntax for the `text-shadow` property is given as follows:

```
text-shadow: <color><offset-x><offset-y><blur-radius>;
```

The word-wrap property

The `word-wrap` property is used by the browser to break lines within the words to prevent the text from exceeding the boundary, or else it will exceed the boundary. It forces the text to wrap, even if it has to split it in the middle of a word.

Syntax

The syntax for the `word-wrap` property is given as:

```
word-wrap:break-word / normal;
```

Values

The values of the `word-wrap` property are as follows:

- `word-break`: This allows unbreakable words to be broken
- `normal`: This breaks words only at the allowed break points

Some new text properties which CSS3 provides are as follows:

- `hanging-punctuation`: This specifies whether a punctuation character can be placed outside the line box or not
- `punctuation-trim`: This specifies whether a punctuation character should be trimmed or not
- `text-align-last`: This describes how the last line of a block or a line right before a forced line break is aligned
- `text-emphasis`: This applies emphasis marks to the element's text and the foreground color to the emphasis marks
- `text-justify`: This specifies the justification method used when `text-align` is `justify`
- `text-outline`: This specifies the outline of the text
- `text-overflow`: This specifies what action needs to be taken when the text overflows in the containing element
- `text-wrap`: This specifies the line-breaking rules for the text
- `word-break`: For non-CJK scripts, this specifies the line-breaking rules

Fonts

In CSS2, the fonts module is used to define size, line height, and weight of a text, as well as other properties such as style and family.

In CSS we could use only predefined font families that were available on the computer, but CSS3 gives us the facility to use user-defined fonts which can be used to style the web forms.

The @font-face rule

Fonts play a major role in deciding how a page or a particular part of a page looks, and that's where the web designers and corporates take benefit, such as in the case of branding.

The `@font-face` property has taken the usage of fonts to the next level.

This rule allows users to specify any real fonts to the text on the web forms or page. To be more precise, this rule allows downloading a particular font from the server and using it in the web form or page if the user hasn't got that particular font already installed.

Syntax

The syntax for the @font-face property is as follows:

```
@font-face{
  font-family: <family-name>;
  src: <url>;
  unicode-range: <urange>;
  font-variant: <font-variant>;
  font-feature-settings: normal / <feature-tag-value>;
  font-stretch: <font-stretch>;
  font-weight: <weight>;
  font-style: <style>;
}
```

Font descriptors

CSS3 provides new font descriptors that can be defined inside the @font-face rule. Various font descriptors that can be used are as follows.

The src font descriptor

The src font descriptor is used to define the URL of the font.

Value: URL.

The font-style font descriptor

The font-style font descriptor is used to define the style of the font that is to be used. It is an optional field and the default is normal.

Values: normal, italic, and oblique.

The font-stretch font descriptor

The font-stretch font descriptor is used to define how much the font should be stretched. It is an optional field and the default is normal.

Value: normal, condensed, ultra-condensed, extra-condensed, semi-condensed, expanded, semi-expanded, extra-expanded, and ultra-expanded.

The font-family font descriptor

The font-family font descriptor is used to define the name or type of the font.

Value: name.

The unicode-range font descriptor

The unicode-range font descriptor is used to define the range of Unicode characters that the font supports. It is an optional field and by default its value is U+0-10FFFF.

Value: Unicode-range.

The font-weight descriptor

The font-weight font descriptor is used to define how bold the font should be. It is an optional field and by default it is normal.

Values: normal, bold, 100, 200, 300, 400, 500, 600, 700, 800, and 900.

Gradients

One of CSS3's amazing color feature is gradients. They allow a smooth transition from one color to another.

They are declared using the background-image property as they have no special property.

Gradients allow us to create transparency by translating the color hex to rgba mode.

In spite of many enhancements, vendor prefixes are used to make the form browser compatible so the browser can interpret the styles.

Syntax

The syntax for gradients is as follows:

```
linear-gradient (<angle><to [left / right || top / bottom]><color
    [percentage/length]><color [percentage/length]>)
```

Values

The values of gradients include the following:

- angle: This specifies the gradient's angle of direction
- color: This specifies the color value with an optional option of stop position

Styling the forms

After a quick revision of the new CSS3 properties, it's time to customize the old and boring forms.

In *Chapter 1, Forms and Their Significance*, we built a **Health Survey Form**. We will reuse that form example to talk about the new CSS3 as well as the basic CSS properties and how they work to enhance the creativity in the form.

For styling, we will just take the first part of the form which is **Personal Information**. With some minor changes which need no explanation, the following is the HTML code:

```
<form id="masteringhtml5_form">
  <label for="heading" class="heading">Health Survey Form</label>
  <fieldset class="fieldset_border">
    <legend class="legend">Personal Information</legend>
    <div>
      <label for="name">Name</label><br>
      <input type="text" class="name txtinput" name="name"
        placeholder="First" autofocus>
      <input type="text" class="name txtinput" name="name"
        placeholder="Last">
    </div><br>
    <div class="div_outer_dob">
      <div class="div_dob">
        <label for="dob">Date of Birth</label><br>
        <input type="date" value="date of birth" class="txtinput
          dateinput">
      </div>
      <div class="gender">
        <label for="gender">Gender</label><br>
        <input type="radio" name="gender"><label>Male</label>
        <input type="radio" name="gender"><label>Female</label>
      </div>
    </div>

    <div class="div_outer_address" >
      <label for="address">Address</label><br>
      <input type="text" class="txtinput textbox address_img"
        placeholder="Street Address"><br>
      <input type="text" class="txtinput textbox address_img"
        placeholder="Address Line 2"><br>
      <input type="text" class="txtinput  address_img"
        placeholder="City">
```

```
      <input type="text" class="txtinput  address_img"
        placeholder="State/Province"><br>
      <input type="text" class="txtinput  address_img"
        placeholder="Pincode">
      <select class="txtinput select address_img" >
        <option value="Country" class="select"  >Select
          Country</option>
        <option value="India" class="select"  >India</option>
        <option value="Australia" class="select"
          >Australia</option>
      </select>
    </div><br>
    <div>
      <label for="contact">Phone Number</label><br>
      <input type="tel" class="txtinput  home_tel"
        placeholder="Home">
      <input type="tel" class="txtinput  work_tel"
        placeholder="Work">
    </div><br>
    <div>
      <label for="email">Email Address</label><br>
      <input type="email" class="txtinput  email"
        placeholder="email@example.com">
    </div>
    </fieldset>
    <br>

  <div class="submit">
    <input type="submit" class="submit_btn" value="Submit">
  </div>
</form>
```

Since our main focus is on styling, let us take a look at the CSS of the form. The following code is maintained in a separate file with a .css extension (external CSS file), which is linked to the main HTML page. Having a separate CSS file should be followed as it improves code readability as well as the maintenance of styling is made easier.

Also, new properties and font types are highlighted in bold:

```
/* General Form */
html{
  margin: 0px;
  padding: 0px;
  background: #000000;
}
```

```css
@font-face{
  font-family: 'Conv_azoft-sans-bold-italic';
  src: url('fonts/azoft-sans-bold-italic.eot');
  src: url('fonts/azoft-sans-bold-italic.woff') format('woff'),
  url('fonts/azoft-sans-bold-italic.ttf') format('truetype'),
    url('fonts/azoft-sans-bold-italic.svg') format('svg');
  font-weight: normal;
  font-style: normal;
}

body{
  font-size:12px;
  height: 100%;
  width: 38%;
  padding: 20px;
  margin: 10px auto;
  font-family: Helvetica, Arial, sans-serif;
  color: #000000;
  background: rgba(212,228,239,1);
  background: -moz-linear-gradient(top, rgba(212,228,239,1) 0%,
    rgba(134,174,204,1) 100%);
  background: -webkit-gradient(left top, left bottom, color-
    stop(0%, rgba(212,228,239,1)), color-stop(100%,
    rgba(134,174,204,1)));
  background: -webkit-linear-gradient(top, rgba(212,228,239,1)
    0%, rgba(134,174,204,1) 100%);
  background: -o-linear-gradient(top, rgba(212,228,239,1) 0%,
    rgba(134,174,204,1) 100%);
  background: -ms-linear-gradient(top, rgba(212,228,239,1) 0%,
    rgba(134,174,204,1) 100%);
  background: linear-gradient(to bottom, rgba(212,228,239,1) 0%,
    rgba(134,174,204,1) 100%);
}

input[type="radio"]{
  cursor:pointer;
}

#masteringhtml5_form .fieldset_border{
  border-color:#ffffff;
  border-style: solid;
}

#masteringhtml5_form .txtinput{
```

```css
    font-family: Helvetica, Arial, sans-serif;
    border-style: solid;
    border-radius: 4px;
    border-width: 1px;
    border-color: #dedede;
    font-size: 18px;
    padding-left: 40px;
    width: 40%;
    color: #777;
    cursor:pointer;
}

#masteringhtml5_form .name{
    background: #fff url('images/user.png')  no-repeat;
}

#masteringhtml5_form  label{
    font-weight:bold;
    font-size:17px;
}

#masteringhtml5_form .legend{
    font-size: 18px;
    font-family: 'Conv_azoft-sans-bold-italic',Helvetica, Arial,
        sans-serif;
}

#masteringhtml5_form .heading{
    font-size: 24px;
    font-family: 'Conv_azoft-sans-bold-italic',Helvetica, Arial,
        sans-serif;
}

#masteringhtml5_form .txtinput.textbox{
    width:89%;
}

#masteringhtml5_form .address_img{
    background: #fff url('images/home.png')  no-repeat;
    background-position-y: -5px;
}

#masteringhtml5_form .txtinput.select{
```

```css
    width:49%;
    color:#777777;
}

#masteringhtml5_form .div_outer_dob{
    width:100%;
}

#masteringhtml5_form .dateinput{
    width:79%;
    background: #fff url('images/date.png')  no-repeat;
    background-position-x: 1px;
    background-size: 29px 29px;
}

#masteringhtml5_form .home_tel{
    background: #fff url('images/tel.png')  no-repeat;
    background-position-x: 1px;
    background-size: 29px 29px;
}

#masteringhtml5_form .work_tel{
    background: #fff url('images/work.png')  no-repeat;
    background-size: 27px 25px;
}

#masteringhtml5_form .email{
    background: #fff url('images/email.png')  no-repeat;
}

#masteringhtml5_form .div_dob{
    width:50%;
    float:left;
}

#masteringhtml5_form .gender{
    width:50%;
    float:left;
}

#masteringhtml5_form .gender span{
    font-size:18px;
}
```

```
#masteringhtml5_form .div_outer_address{
  clear:both;
}

.legend{
  font-weight:bold;
  font-size:14px;
}

#masteringhtml5_form .submit{
  text-align:center;
}

#masteringhtml5_form .submit_btn{
  color:#ffffff;
  cursor:pointer;
  border-radius:5px;
  width: 17%;
  height: 100%;
  font-size: 21px;
  height:100%;
  box-shadow: 5px 5px 10px 5px #888888;
  background: rgb(149,149,149);
  background: -moz-linear-gradient(top,  rgba(149,149,149,1) 0%,
    rgba(13,13,13,1) 46%, rgba(1,1,1,1) 50%, rgba(10,10,10,1)
    53%, rgba(78,78,78,1) 76%, rgba(56,56,56,1) 87%,
    rgba(27,27,27,1) 100%);
  background: -webkit-gradient(linear, left top, left bottom,
    color-stop(0%,rgba(149,149,149,1)), color-
    stop(46%,rgba(13,13,13,1)), color-stop(50%,rgba(1,1,1,1)),
    color-stop(53%,rgba(10,10,10,1)), color-
    stop(76%,rgba(78,78,78,1)), color-stop(87%,
    rgba(56,56,56,1)), color-stop(100%,rgba(27,27,27,1)));
  background: -webkit-linear-gradient(top,  rgba(149,149,149,1)
    0%,rgba(13,13,13,1) 46%,rgba(1,1,1,1) 50%,rgba(10,10,10,1)
    53%,rgba(78,78,78,1) 76%,rgba(56,56,56,1) 87%,
    rgba(27,27,27,1) 100%);
  background: -o-linear-gradient(top,  rgba(149,149,149,1)
    0%,rgba(13,13,13,1) 46%,rgba(1,1,1,1) 50%,rgba(10,10,10,1)
    53%,rgba(78,78,78,1) 76%,rgba(56,56,56,1) 87%,
    rgba(27,27,27,1) 100%);
  background: -ms-linear-gradient(top,  rgba(149,149,149,1)
    0%,rgba(13,13,13,1) 46%,rgba(1,1,1,1) 50%,rgba(10,10,10,1)
    53%,rgba(78,78,78,1) 76%,rgba(56,56,56,1) 87%,
    rgba(27,27,27,1) 100%);
```

```
background: linear-gradient(to bottom,   rgba(149,149,149,1)
   0%,rgba(13,13,13,1) 46%,rgba(1,1,1,1) 50%,rgba(10,10,10,1)
   53%,rgba(78,78,78,1) 76%,rgba(56,56,56,1) 87%,
   rgba(27,27,27,1) 100%);
}
```

The result of the previous HTML and CSS code is as follows:

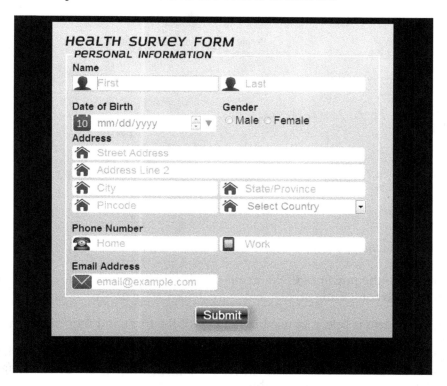

If we compare the new CSS3 form with the first section of the form which we built in *Chapter 1, Forms and Their Significance,* we will see the difference in the look and feel of both the forms.

For better comparison, the first section of the form in *Chapter 1, Forms and Their Significance*, is given as follows:

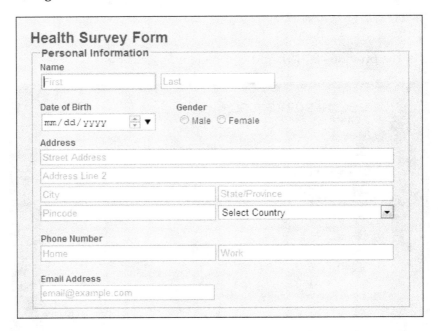

Now, we realize the power of CSS3, using which we have converted a simple and boring form into something stylish and eye catching very easily.

Let us see the various selectors used in the CSS of the form and their significance:

- `<body>`: The CSS attributes applied to the `<body>` tag acts as a fallback or default attribute as it acts as the parent tag containing several other tags inside it. The `fallback` attributes for CSS are `font-family`, `font-size`, and so on.

An attribute such as `background` which utilizes the color (in terms of RBG), is set with the help of `linear-gradient`. The `linear-gradient` is described with the help of RBG color value, starting from the top with stop values defined as percentage till the bottom. They are described for the different browser supports which contain start values such as `-webkit`, `-O`, "and" `-ms`. It shows the blue background of the form. Apart from this, various other CSS attributes such as `font-size`, `height`, and `width` are also used.

- `heading` and `legend`: For our form heading (**Health Survey Form**) and legend heading (**Personal Information**), we have implemented a new font type, `Conv_azoft-sans-bold-italic`, which is defined in the `font-family` attribute in the `heading` and `legend` class using the `@font-face` property.

  We have imported the font type files `.eot`, `.woff`, `.ttf`, and `.svg` for supporting different browsers with the help of the `@font-face` property.

  Also, for the `legend` tag we have utilized the `fieldset_border` class for changing the border color and style.

- `dateinput` and `div_dob`: Both these classes are defined for the `<input>` type date for the user to pick his/her date of birth from the drop-down calendar. The `div_dob` class is defined for the arrangement of the elements on the screen by utilizing the `float` attribute one the left-hand side. Along with it, the `dateinput` class is used for placing the date icon with the help of the `background`, `background-position`, and `background-size` properties for proper rendering.

- `txtinput`: The `txtinput` class is used for styling the text inputs used in the form, and apart from using the previous CSS attributes, such as `font-family` and `border-style`, we have used a new attribute named `border-radius` to give the text input a rounded border on all sides.

  We have also added a property for the `cursor` type as a pointer that shows a hand-click icon when we move the mouse pointer over the input field.

  The classes `name`, `address_img`, `home_tel`, `work_tel`, `email`, `dropdown`, and `calendar` have been used for setting the background image for the text inputs fields with their respective icon images depending on the `<input>` type. We have utilized various properties of the background, such as `background`, `background-position`, and `background-size` for proper rendering of an icon image.

  The `autofocus` attribute is used on the first name text input for the automatic focus of the cursor during the form load.

- `radiobutton`: The `<input>` type `radio` is an old HTML input, which is used here for the purpose of selecting the gender. We have also used the `float` property for aligning the radio buttons on the right-hand side of the date of birth.

  We have also added a property for the `cursor` type as a pointer that shows a hand-click icon when we move the mouse pointer over the input field.

- `submit`: For submitting the form to the server, we have created a **Submit** button. In the `submit_btn` class we have performed button customization using the previous version properties such as color, width, and height, along with CSS3 properties such as `border-radius` to round the button from all sides, `box-shadow`, and `background` with a color attribute using `linear-gradients` to provide the desired effect.

  We have also added a property for the `cursor` type which is a pointer that shows a hand-click icon when we move the mouse pointer over the input field.

Guidelines

In this section, we will see the CSS3 guidelines for effective styling of the forms.

Some of the best practices for CSS3 are as follows:

- Avoid using inline styling for CSS. External CSS files must be used for styling.
- Minified CSS files must be used wherever possible as this a practice for removing unnecessary characters from the code to reduce the size.
- Use combined files for CSS.
- Avoid use of multiple declarations wherever possible.
- Always think of progressive enhancement.
- Vendor prefixes should be organized and well commented.
- For background-related properties use fallback.
- The readability of the text should not be affected while using typography.
- Enable the fallback and test the form in every browser.
- Try to use efficient CSS selectors.
- Avoid the usage of CSS Expression wherever possible.
- Specify image dimensions to improve the rendering speed of the web page.
- Use CSS sprites for faster rendering of images.

Summary

In this chapter, we learned about the basics of CSS3 and the modules in which we can categorize the CSS3 for forms, such as vendor prefixes, gradients, and backgrounds.

Then, with the help of a code example, we learned a practical implementation of most of the CSS3 properties that can be used for improving the look and feel of the forms.

Lastly, we learned the best practices for the effective styling of the forms.

4
Connection with Database

In the earlier chapters, we learned about forms, such as what forms are, how we can validate them, and how we can improve the look and feel of them, but what is the use of forms until they store information? In this chapter, we will learn how to store the user's input data into a database using PHP and MySQL.

In this chapter, we will cover the following topics:

- What is PHP
- What is MySQL
- Spoofing and forging forms
- Linking of forms to the database

PHP

PHP, which is also used as a general-purpose programming language, is basically a server-side scripting language, which is designed for web development. With a PHP processor module, PHP code is interpreted by a web server resulting in the generation of a web page.

Rather than calling an external file to process data, PHP commands can be embedded directly into the HTML code. It can be used for standalone graphical applications and can be deployed on most of the web servers for almost every operating system and platform.

All variables in PHP are case-sensitive, but user-defined functions, classes, and keywords such as if, else, while, echo, and many more are case-insensitive.

On the server, first a PHP script is executed and then the HTML result is sent back to the browser.

Through an HTML form, the ability of PHP to easily manipulate the information submitted by the user is one of the reasons why it is popular.

To use PHP, we have to perform the following steps:

1. Get a web server that supports PHP and MySQL.

2. In this chapter, we will use WAMP (used for Windows operating systems) software, which automatically installs the Apache server, configures a MySQL database, and installs PHP-support applications for easy maintenance and configuration.

3. Then, install PHP and MySQL.

Syntax

The default extension for a PHP file is .php and a PHP script starts with <?php and ends with ?>.

```
<?php
  // PHP script
?>
```

Including some PHP scripting code, a PHP file normally contains HTML tags. A semicolon is used to terminate PHP statements, and we do not need to use a semicolon to terminate the last line of a PHP block.

Form handling

The $_GET and $_POST PHP superglobals (built-in variables that are always available in all scopes) are used to collect the form data which is submitted by the user on clicking on the **Submit** button.

The GET method

In the GET method, the information from a form is visible to everyone; for example, all the variable names and the values are displayed in the URL. Moreover, using the GET method has limits on the amount of information that can be sent, which varies from browser to browser.

This method is useful when we need to bookmark the web page because the variables are displayed in the URL.

We cannot use the GET method for sending sensitive data, such as passwords or credit card information.

The following code is a simple HTML page:

```
<html>
<body>
<form action="example.php" method="get">
  Name: <input type="text" name="name"><br>
  Age: <input type="text" name="age"><br>
  <input type="submit">
</form>
</body>
</html>
```

When a user fills the preceding form and clicks on the **Submit** button, the form data is sent for processing to a PHP file named example.php. The form data is sent with method="get".

The example.php file will look similar to the following code:

```
<html>
<body>
  Hello! <?php echo $_GET["name"]; ?>!<br>
  You are <?php echo $_GET["age"]; ?> years old.
</body>
</html>
```

The POST method

The information from a form is not visible to everyone in the POST method; for example, within the body of the HTTP request, all the variable names and the values are embedded. Moreover, using the POST method has no limitation on the amount of information to send.

This method is not useful when we need to bookmark the web page because the variables are not displayed in the URL.

Moreover, while uploading the files to the server, the POST method also supports advanced functionality such as support for multipart binary input.

We can use the POST method for sending sensitive data, such as passwords or credit card information.

The following code is a simple HTML page:

```html
<html>
<body>
<form action="example.php" method="post">
  Name: <input type="text" name="name"><br>
  Age: <input type="text" name="age"><br>
  <input type="submit">
</form>
</body>
</html>
```

When a user fills the preceding form and clicks on the submit button, the form data is sent for processing to a PHP file named example.php. The form data is sent with method="post".

The example.php file looks like this:

```php
<html>
<body>
  Hello! <?php echo $_POST["name"]; ?>!<br>
  You are <?php echo $_POST["age"]; ?> years old.
</body>
</html>
```

Both the GET and POST methods populate the $_GET and $_POST arrays respectively. As these are superglobals, regardless of scope, they are always accessible, and they can be accessed from any class, function, or file without having to do anything special. These arrays are described as follows:

- $_GET: This is an array of variable, via the URL parameters is passed to the current script

- $_POST: This is an array of variable, via the HTTP POST method is passed to the current script

 POST is the most preferred way to send form data because of security concerns.

The filter method

The filter method filters data by either validating or sanitizing the input fields. It plays a very important role and is useful when the data source contains unknown data, such as custom input or user supplied input.

For example, data entered through an HTML form in cases, such as survey forms, and new registrations.

There are two main types of filtering:

- Validation
- Sanitization

Filtering of input data is one of the major concerns when it comes to security issues. External data includes input data from the user, cookies, web service data, or database query results. As all web forms and applications depend on external input so with filtering the input data we can be sure that our application gets valid input from the user.

The following `filter` functions can be used to filter a variable:

- `filter_var_array()`: It gets multiple variables with the same or different filters
- `filter_id()`: It returns the ID number of a specified filter
- `filter_var()`: It filters a single variable with a specified filter
- `filter_input()`: It gets one input variable by the name and optionally filters it
- `filter_has_var()`: It checks whether a variable of a specified input type exists or not
- `filter_input_array()`: It gets several input variables and filters them with the same or different filters
- `filter_list()`: It returns a list of all the supported filters

In the following example, we are validating an integer using the `filter_var()` function:

```php
<?php
  $int = 'g819';
  if(!filter_var($int, FILTER_VALIDATE_INT))
  {
    echo("Entered integer is invalid");
  }
  else
  {
    echo("Entered integer is valid");
  }
?>
```

In the preceding code, the FILTER_VALIDATE_INT filter is used to filter the variable. Since the integer is not valid, the output of the preceding code will be **Integer is invalid**, but if we try with a variable that is an integer, such as 819, the output will be **Integer is valid**.

Validating user input data

The filter method is used to validate the user input data. It returns the value **true** on success and **false** on failure.

Strict format rules are followed for validating the IP address, URL, variables, or e-mail type.

Now, in the following example, we will validate an input field of a form. Before we start, we will first check the presence of the required input data. Then, using the filter_var() function, we will validate the input data.

```php
<?php
if(!filter_has_var($_GET["url"]))
{
  echo("Input type is not present");
}
else
{
if (!filter_var($_GET["url"], FILTER_VALIDATE_URL))
{
  echo "Entered URL is invalid";
}
else
{
  echo "Entered URL is valid";
}
}
?>
```

In the preceding example, an input url is sent using the GET method. It first checks if an input email variable of the GET type is present or not. When the input variable is present, it validates the URL.

Sanitizing user input data

The main purpose of sanitizing is to allow or not to allow the specified characters in the string. It always returns a string value. It does not follow any data format rules.

In the following example, we will validate an input field of a form. Before we start, we will first check the presence of the required input data. Then, using the filter_var() function, we will sanitize the input data.

```php
<?php
  if(!filter_has_var(($_POST['string'])
  {
    echo("Input type is not present");
  }
  else
  {
    $string = filter_var($_POST['string'],
      FILTER_SANITIZE_STRING);
  }
?>
```

In the preceding example, an input string is sent using the POST method. It first checks if an input string variable of the POST type exists. When the input variable is present, it validates the string.

When the user inputs a bad input string such as MasteringååHTML5ååForms, after sanitizing, the same string will look like MasteringHTML5Form.

The FILTER_CALLBACK filter

Using the FILTER_CALLBACK filter, it is possible to call a user-defined function and use it as a filter. We can get full control of data filtering using this.

In a similar manner as when specifying an option, the function which we want to use to filter is specified.

We can use an existing PHP function or also create our own user-defined functions.

In the following example, we will create a user-defined function to replace all * symbols with whitespaces:

```php
<?php
  function towhitespace($string)
  {
```

```
        return str_replace("*", " ", $string);
    }
    $string = "Converting*To*Whitespace*Characters";
    echo filter_var($string, FILTER_CALLBACK,
    array("options"=>"towhitespace"));
?>
```

The output of the preceding code is:

Converting To Whitespace Characters

In the preceding example, at any place in a string and no matter how many times, all the * symbols are replaced with the whitespace characters.

In the preceding code, we first created a function to replace all the * symbols with whitespaces. Then, the filter_var() function is called with the FILTER_CALLBACK filter and an array containing the function.

Filter multiple inputs

Nowadays, almost every web form consists of more than one input field such as the registration page. When a form consists of more than one input field, calling filter_var() or filter_input() functions for every input field to validate or sanitize not only increases the size of the code but also the complexity. The remedy for this is to use the filter_var_array() or filter_input_array() functions.

In the following example, we will validate two input fields of a form. We will use the filter_var_array() function to filter these variables and use the POST method. The input is in the form of age and e-mail address.

```
<?php
  $filters = array
  (
    "age" => array
    (
      "filter"=>FILTER_VALIDATE_INT,
      "options"=>array
        (
        "min_range"=>1,
        "max_range"=>99
      )
    ),
    "email"=> FILTER_VALIDATE_EMAIL
  );
```

```
$output = filter_var_array($_POST, $filters);

if (!$output["age"])
{
    echo("Entered age must be between 1 and 99");
}
elseif(!$output["email"])
{
    echo("Entered email is invalid");
}
else
{
    echo("Entered inputs are valid");
}
?>
```

In the preceding example, the input fields are sent using the POST method. Here, an array is set, which contains the name of the input variables, such as age and email. We have also used the filters on these input variables.

First, we call the filter_var_array() function with the POST method input variables and the array we had set. Then, we validated the age and email variables in the $output variable for the invalid inputs.

The second parameter of the filter_input_array() or filter_var_array() function can be a single filter ID or an array. All the values in the input array are filtered by the specified filter when the parameter is a single filter ID.

The following rules must be followed if the parameter is an array:

- The array value must be a filter ID or an array specifying the flags, filters, and options
- There must be an associative array that contains an input variable as an array key, such as the email or age input variable

MySQL

A database is a structured and organized collection of data. Every frontend application needs a compatible database which works as a backend for the application. It is organized for efficient storage and retrieval based on the nature of the data rather than the collection or retrieval methods. Adding a database to a website provides the means for dynamic content, flexibility and manageability, and all kinds of user interactivity, which without this could not be easily accomplished.

To work with the corresponding data, database management system applications interact with the user, other applications, and the database itself. This application will work as a backend for managing all data. There are many well-known DBMSes, which include Microsoft SQL Server, Oracle, Sybase, MySQL, PostgreSQL, SQLite, Microsoft Access, dBASE, FoxPro, IBM's DB2, Libre Office Base, and FileMaker Pro.

MySQL for PHP

When working with PHP, MySQL is the most compatible database system. This database
is an essential part of almost every open source PHP application.

MySQL is named after *My*, daughter of *Michael Widenius*, co-founder of MySQL. It is developed, distributed, and supported by Oracle Corporation. It is a freely available and easy-to-download open source database management system. It is very fast, reliable, and supports standard **Structured Query Language** (SQL).

SQL is used to access and modify data or information from a storage area called a database. It is most noted for its quick processing, proven reliability, and ease and flexibility of use. Developed by IBM, it is an English-like language that processes data in groups of records rather than one record at a time. The following are a few of the functions of SQL:

- Storing data
- Modifying data
- Retrieving data
- Deleting data
- Creating tables and other database objects

The data in MySQL is stored in tables. A table is a collection of related data, and all data is arranged in columns and rows. Databases are useful when storing information categorically.

MySQL-PHP connectivity

While working with any database, the first question that arises is "How can we access data from the database?" To access any database, we first have to connect to that database.

Open a connection to the MySQL server

To make a connection, we first have to open a connection to the MySQL server. In PHP, this is done with the `mysqli_connect()` function. This function returns a resource which is a pointer to the database connection. It's also called a database handle.

The syntax for the `mysqli_connect()` function is:

```
mysqli_connect(server,username,password,dbname);
```

It supports the following values:

* `server`: It is either an IP address or a hostname.
* `password`: It is the password to log in with and is optional.
* `username`: It is the MySQL username and is optional. Also, MySQL can have multiple users.
* `dbname`: It is the default database to be used when performing queries and is optional.

For example:

```php
<?php
  $username = "your_name";
  $password = "your_password";
  $hostname = "localhost";
  $dbname = "your_db";
  $dbconnect = mysqli_connect($hostname, $username, $password,
    $dbname)
  //Connects to the database
?>
```

Close a connection

PHP will automatically close the connection when the script ends. But if we want to close the connection before it ends, we use the `mysqli_close()` function.

For example:

```php
<?php
  mysqli_close($dbhandle);
  //Closes the connection
?>
```

Create or select a database

Once our connection to a database is successfully created, the next step is to create or select any database that is going to be used with our application.

Create a database

For creating a database, we use the CREATE DATABASE statement to create a database table in MySQL.

For example:

```php
<?php
  $createDB="CREATE DATABASE personal_info";
  //Creates a database with name as "personal_info"

  mysqli_query($createDB)
  //Executes the create database query
?>
```

Select a database

For selecting an already present database, we use the MYSQLI_SELECT_DB statement to select a database in MySQL.

For example:

```php
<?php
  $dbconnect = mysqli_connect("host name", "username",
    "password", "dbname")
  //Connects to the database

  $dbselected = mysqli_select_db("personal_info",$dbconnect)
  //Selects the database to work with
?>
```

Create a table

Once we create or select a database, the next step is to create a table inside the database.

CREATE TABLE is used to create a table in MySQL.

For example:

```php
<?php
  $createTB="CREATE TABLE TbDummy(
    Firstname VARCHAR(255) NOT NULL,
    Lastname VARCHAR(255) NOT NULL);
  //Creating a table in MySQL with name as "TbDummy"

  mysqli_query($createTB)
  //Executing the create table query
?>
```

Primary keys

To increase flexibility and reliability in a table, the primary key field must be present.

A table consists of many records and to uniquely identify each record, a primary key is used. Each record must have one value that is unique, and that unique value will act as the primary key. Also, a primary key value cannot be null, as to locate a record, the database engine requires a value. A primary key is a combination of columns, which uniquely identifies a record.

For example:

Let's look at the Employee table that contains a record for each employee working in an organization:

Employee ID	Name	Designation	Location
101	Gaurav Gupta	Programmer Analyst	Pune
102	Gaurav Gupta	Programmer Analyst	Pune

The table consists of two records with the same name, designation, and location. The employee's unique Employee ID number will be a good choice for a primary key in the Employee table. So, we set the column Employee ID as a primary key for this table.

The following snippet is a sample code to create a table by defining a column as a primary key:

```php
<?php
  $createDB="CREATE DATABASE DBEmployee";
  //Creates a database with name as "DBEmployee"
```

```
mysqli_query($createDB)
//Executes the create database query

$createTB="CREATE TABLE Employee(
  Employee_ID INT NOT NULL,
  Name VARCHAR(255),
  Designation VARCHAR(255),
  Location VARCHAR(255),
  PRIMARY KEY(Employee_ID));
//Creating a table with name as "Employee" and defining
  a column "Employee_ID" as a primary key

mysqli_query($createTB)
//Executing the create table query
?>
```

Spoofing and forging forms

Nowadays, every website has an HTML form to complete for registration so that users can have access to that particular website. Since Internet crime is steadily increasing, how do we validate that the user who completed the form did so through your website? It is therefore necessary to know that no one has spoofed our form submission.

Before, we see how we can protect our forms from spoofing, let us see how we can spoof a form. By following these two ways we can alter the form submission:

- Forging HTTP requests
- Spoofing submissions

Forging HTTP requests

We can type our own requests by using telnet to access port 80. So, botheration of generating or modifying forms for every type of attack is overcome by this method as it might just use raw HTTP for alteration of form data. Because of this, we can say that this method has a higher degree of complexity than others.

Forging HTTP requests is a more advanced form of automating attacks.

In the following example, we are requesting to log in to the example forum:

```
POST /index.php?act=Login&CODE=01&CookieDate=1 HTTP/1.1
Host: forums.example.com
Connection: close
```

```
Referrer: http://forums.example.com/
Cookie: session_id=7819
Content-Type: application/x-www-form-urlencoded
Content-Length: 44

UserName=myname&PassWord=mypass&CookieDate=1
```

To use the preceding mentioned requests, you will need to change a few items, which are:

- Change `myname` to be our username
- Change `mypass` to be our password
- Change `session_id` to the necessary value
- Change `Content-Length` to be the new length of the POST data

Spoofing submissions

Let us assume that the following HTML form is located at `http://sampledomain.com/form.php`:

```html
<form action="/example.php" method="post">
  <select name="browser">
  <option value="chrome">Chrome</option>
  <option value="firefox">Firefox</option>
  </select>
  <input type="submit">
</form>
```

We assume that we will be able to refer to `$_POST['browser']` and it will have a value of either of the two options `chrome` or `firefox`. Now, if the user selects `chrome`,
the request will look something similar to the following:

```
POST /example.php HTTP/1.1
Host: sampledomain.com
Content-Type: application/x-www-form-urlencoded
Content-Length: 8

browser=chrome
```

A user can save the form from the browser to the local machine (desktop or laptop) then open the saved HTML file and make the following changes to it:

- Modify the `action` tag so that it now has the full URL to the form
- Remove the `select` tag and replace it with a `textarea` tag in the form

Now our form will look similar to the following code:

```
<form action=http://sampledomain.com/example.php method="post">
  <textarea name="myvar"></textarea>
  <input type="submit">
</form>
```

The user can now submit any value of `$_POST['myvar']` with these simple changes to the form. Moreover, there is no way to prevent the user who manipulated our form from submitting unexpected form variables or anything that can be achieved with an HTML form.

There are solutions available to prevent forms from spoofing. It is from a strict protocol perspective; the only thing we know is that HTTP requests and responses are going back and forth. There is no clear and concise way to determine that a form submission has not been spoofed.

Using the following two ways, we can prevent forms from spoofing as they reduce the possibility of unwanted values that are submitted by following a general architecture for handling data and forms:

- Shared secrets
- Setting expectations

Shared secrets

Shared secrets are also referred to as one-time tokens or hashes. We create a secret that is only known by the server and the user. In this, the implementations vary widely but they share the characteristics of being transparent to the users and are difficult to exploit.

One of the implementation methods is that in the user's session, we will store the secret as shown in the following code:

```
$secret = md5(uniqid(rand(), true));
$_SESSION['secret'] = $secret;
```

Now, it can be used as a hidden form variable in the form like:

```
<input type="hidden" name="secret" value="<?
  echo $secret; ?>" />
```

Every time we display the form, we would regenerate this secret so that the user always has a current and correct secret value. This helps in preventing **CSRF (Cross-Site Request Forgery)**.

The page which will open can check this by comparing the secret sent by the form with the secret that was stored in the corresponding session variable.

Taking this further, we can even enhance the security of this method by restricting the timeout window rather than relying on the session timeout, which can be too large for your needs.

Setting expectations

An application with a best architecture always assumes that:

- **We are aware of what we are sending out**: It means we should keep track of the forms we have uploaded on the website and develop a policy for accepting form submissions, such as time outs, multiple forms per user ID, multiple submissions, and not accepting forms we don't expect. This can be implemented using tokens.

- **We are aware of what the return values will be**: It is important, as the <select> field contains certain values, we can get back something totally different, such as PHP code, SQL, or others:

    - To accept the form as valid, we must know the fields we need to have back
    - We must restrict exactly what values we would accept as input
    - We must always minimize taking data from forms or from an external source and using it directly in our database queries or other internal parts of the application

Linking a form to a server

The basic purpose of form is to accept user data or store data from the users, which can be accessed in various ways, such as a survey, a new registration, while making payments, and much more. So here, in this section, we will learn how to store the user's input data into the database.

We will reuse our form which we styled in *Chapter 3, Styling the Forms*.

We will store the form data into a MySQL database using phpMyAdmin (open sourcetool to handle the administration of MySQL over World Wide Web).

For operating systems such as Linux, we use a XAMPP server.

The following is the server-side scripting code written in the same HTML page but the HTML file extension .html is changed to .php:

```php
<?php
  mysqli_connect("localhost", "root", "");

  mysqli_select_db("DBpersonal_info");
  if(isset($_REQUEST['submit']))
  {
    $errorMessage = "";
    $Gender ="";
    $Firstname=$_POST['Firstname'];
    $Lastname=$_POST['Lastname'];
    $Dob=$_POST['Dob'];
    $Gender=$_POST['Gender'];
    $Saddress=$_POST['Saddress'];
    $City=$_POST['City'];
    $State=$_POST['State'];
    $Pincode=$_POST['Pincode'];
    $Country=$_POST['Country'];
    $Home=$_POST['Home'];
    $Work=$_POST['Work'];
    $Email=$_POST['Email'];
    $Aaddress = $_POST['Aaddress'];

    //Field validation
    if(empty($Firstname)) {
      $errorMessage .= "<li>You forgot to enter a first
      name!</li>";
    }
    if(empty($Lastname)) {
      $errorMessage .= "<li>You forgot to enter a last
      name!</li>";
    }
    if(empty($Dob)) {
      $errorMessage .= "<li>You forgot to select a date of
      birth!</li>";
    }
    if(empty($Gender)) {
      $errorMessage .= "<li>You forgot to select your
      Gender!</li>";
    }
    if(empty($Saddress)) {
      $errorMessage .= "<li>You forgot to enter street
```

```
  address!</li>";
}
if(empty($City)) {
  $errorMessage .= "<li>You forgot to enter city!</li>";
}
if(empty($State)) {
  $errorMessage .= "<li>You forgot to enter state!</li>";
}
if(empty($Pincode)) {
  $errorMessage .= "<li>You forgot to enter pincode!</li>";
}
if(empty($Country)) {
   $errorMessage .= "<li>You forgot to select country!</li>";
}
if(empty($Home)) {
   $errorMessage .= "<li>You forgot to enter home phone
   number!</li>";
}
if(empty($Work)) {
  $errorMessage .= "<li>You forgot to enter work phone
  number!</li>";
}
if(empty($Email)) {
  $errorMessage .= "<li>You forgot to enter email id!</li>";
}

//Check if the number field is numeric
if(is_numeric(trim($Pincode)) == false ) {
$errorMessage .= "<li>Please enter numeric pincode
  value!</li>";
}
if(is_numeric(trim($Home)) == false ) {
  $errorMessage .= "<li>Please enter numeric home phone
    number!</li>";
}
if(is_numeric(trim($Work)) == false ) {
  $errorMessage .= "<li>Please enter numeric work
    phone number!</li>";
}

//Check if the length of field is upto required
if(strlen($Pincode)!=6) {
  $errorMessage .= "<li>Pincode should be 6 digits
    only!</li>";
}
```

```
if(strlen($Work)!=10) {
  $errorMessage .= "<li>Work phone number should be 10 digits
  only!</li>";
}

//Check for valid email format
if(!filter_var($Email, FILTER_VALIDATE_EMAIL)) {
  $errorMessage .= "<li>You did not enter a invalid
  email!</li>";
}
    if ($errorMessage != "" ) {
    echo "<p class='message'>" .$errorMessage. "</p>" ;
}
else{
  //Inserting record in table using INSERT query
  $insertTB="INSERT INTO `personal_info`.`personal`
  (`Firstname`, `Lastname`, `Dob`, `Gender`, `Saddress`,
  `Aaddress`, `City`, `State`, `Pincode`, `Country`, `Home`,
  `Work`, `Email`) VALUES ('$Firstname', '$Lastname', '$Dob',
  '$Gender', '$Saddress', '$Aaddress', '$City', '$State',
  '$Pincode', '$Country', '$Home', '$Work', '$Email')";

  mysqli_query($insertTB);
}
}
?>
```

Before executing the code, our prerequisite is that first we have to create and select one database and then create a table to store the information. After that, we perform some validations on the form inputs, and then finally, we implement the Insert query so as to store the user's input data.

The following screenshot displays the error messages when the user does not enter any data and submits the form:

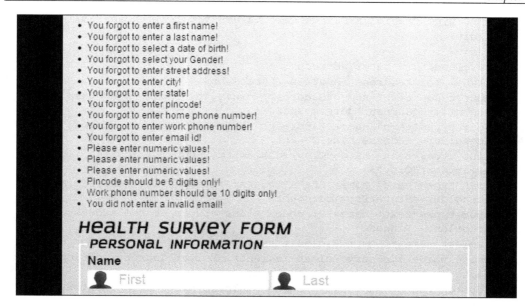

The following is the HTML code. The code remains the same but we have added the `method= "POST"` attribute in the `<form>` tag and the `name` attribute in the `<input>` types:

```
<form id="masteringhtml5_form" method="POST">
<label for="heading" class="heading">Health Survey Form</label>
  <fieldset class="fieldset_border">
  <legend class="legend">Personal Information</legend>
  <div>
  <label for="name">Name</label><br>
<input type="text" name="Firstname" class="name txtinput"
placeholder="First" autofocus>
<input type="text" name="Lastname" class="name txtinput"
placeholder="Last">
  </div><br>
  <div class="div_outer_dob">
  <div class="div_dob">
  <label for="dob">Date of Birth</label><br>
<input type="date" name="Dob" value="date of birth" class="txtinput
dateinput">
  </div>
  <div class="gender">
  <label for="gender">Gender</label><br>
<input type="radio" name="Gender" value="male"> <span>Male</span>
```

```
<input type="radio" name="Gender" value="female"> <span>Female</span>
  </div>
  </div>
<div class="div_outer_address">
  <label for="address">Address</label><br>
<input type="text" name="Saddress" class="txtinput tb address_img"
placeholder="Street Address"><br>
<input type="text" name="Aaddress" class="txtinput tb address_img"
placeholder="Address Line 2"><br>
<input type="text" name="City" class="txtinput tb1 address_img"
placeholder="City">
<input type="text" name="State" class="txtinput tb1 address_img"
placeholder="State/Province"><br>
<input type="text" name="Pincode" class="txtinput tb1 address_img"
placeholder="Pincode">
  <select name="Country" class="txtinput select address_img" >
<option value="Country" class="select" >Select Country</option>
  <option value="India" class="select" >India</option>
  <option value="Australia" class="select" >Australia</option>
  </select>
  </div><br>
  <div>
  <label for="contact">Phone Number</label><br>
<input type="tel" name ="Home" class="txtinput tb1 home_tel"
placeholder="Home">
<input type="tel" name="Work" class="txtinput tb1 work_tel"
placeholder="Work">
  </div><br>
  <div>
  <label for="email">Email Address</label><br>
<input type="email" name="Email" class="txtinput tb1 email"
placeholder="email@example.com">
  </div>
  </fieldset><br>
  <div class="submit">
<input type="submit" name="submit" class="submit_btn" value="Submit">
  </div>
</form>
```

By clicking on the **Submit** button, we can either redirect the user to a new page, or populate a message on the screen, or simply write a message on the screen giving confirmation that our form has been submitted successfully.

The following screenshot displays the form after the user has entered the values in the form:

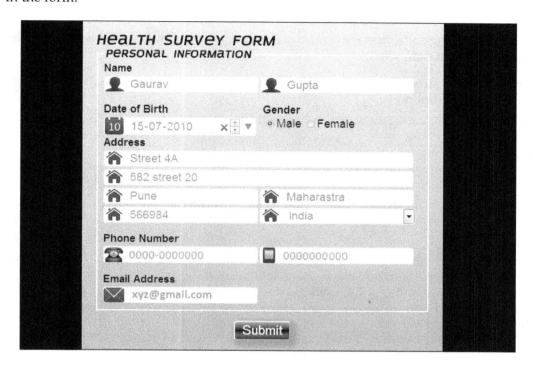

The following snippet is the MySQL code:

```
//Creates database
CREATE DATABASE personal_info

//Creates table
CREATE TABLE personal(
Firstname VARCHAR(255) NOT NULL,
Lastname VARCHAR(255) NOT NULL,
Dob VARCHAR(255) NOT NULL,
Gender VARCHAR(255) NOT NULL,
Saddress VARCHAR(255) NOT NULL,
Aaddress VARCHAR(255) NOT NULL,
City VARCHAR(255) NOT NULL,
State VARCHAR(255) NOT NULL,
Pincode INT(11) NOT NULL,
Country VARCHAR(255) NOT NULL,
```

```
Home VARCHAR(255) NOT NULL,
Work VARCHAR(255) NOT NULL,
Email VARCHAR(255) NOT NULL)
```

In the preceding code, first we created a database and then we created a table to store the user's input data.

The following screenshot displays the values stored into the database after clicking on the **Submit** button:

Summary

In this chapter, we learned how to store data into a database. We also learned about the basics of PHP and MySQL used for storing the data that the users input. We also saw some ways of how we can spoof a form and how we can prevent spoofing of forms.

Then, with the help of some code, we learned a practical implementation of storing form data by reusing the example we built in earlier chapters.

5
Responsive Web Forms

In the previous chapters, we learned about forms: what forms are, how we can validate them, how we can improve the look and feel of a form, and how to store the information collected with the help of forms into a database. But, with the enhancement of technology, different devices with different screen resolutions require different layouts. So, in this chapter we will learn how to make our forms responsive.

In this chapter, we will cover the following topics:

- What is responsive design
- What are media queries
- What are fluid grids
- How to make our forms responsive
- Guidelines for making responsive forms more effective

Responsive design

The term responsive design was introduced in May, 2010, by *Ethan Marcotte*, a writer and web designer, in an article called *Responsive Web Design* that was published on
A List Apart.

Basically, responsive design means how the content is displayed on the various screens, such as mobiles, tablets, or desktops. An approach by which a website or a particular page dynamically adjusts itself according to particular screen resolution to give the best user experience is responsive design. It ensures great user experience as it works independently across various devices and resolutions.

Using fluid, proportion-based grids, flexible images, and CSS3 media queries, a site designed with responsive web design automatically adapts the layout to the particular device resolution.

Web design once used to be simple. Web designers would design for the most popular desktop screen size, create a single layout that works for most of the devices, which allowed us to easily divide our design into a various number of grids so that we can have a well-laid, cohesive, and harmonic page.

But with the enhancements in technology and the introduction of various devices, such as smart phones, tablets, or even mini laptops, the whole experience of web layout and design was changed.

Change in Web has also changed the way people use the Internet. In earlier approaches to web design, it was difficult to use the Internet in mobile devices as the particular website, which was designed for desktops, had scrolling and had to zoom in or out for reading the text and wasting time. For example, pages viewed in a desktop might have links that are text-based and compact which are difficult to click on. But with responsive design, we can tackle these problems with the available features and capabilities of HTML5 and CSS3.

If that website or page were responsive, the text would be larger, all the content would fit on the screen, and the navigation would be mobile-optimized.

The breakpoints in responsive web design are the browser widths that have a media query declaration to change the layout of the website or web page once the declared range is achieved.

Google's view about responsive design

Google recommends building smartphone-optimized sites and it supports the following three configurations:

- The sites which are designed to be responsive serve all devices on the same set of URLs, with each URL rendering the same HTML to all devices and just utilizing CSS to change how the page is rendered on the device
- The sites which dynamically serve all devices with the same set of URLs, but each URL serves different HTML (and CSS) depending on whether the user agent is a desktop or a mobile device
- There are sites which have separate mobile and desktop URLs

Benefits of using responsive design

Some benefits of using responsive designed websites are as follows:

- Using a single URL for a particular content makes it easier for users to interact with, share, and link the content.

- Rather than developing and maintaining multiple websites for desktop and mobile, we just need one website to develop and maintain that works on all kinds of devices.

- Loading time is reduced as no redirection is needed to get the device-optimized view. Moreover, user agent based redirection can degrade a website's user experience and is more error-prone.

- It is future friendly; this means it allows us to adapt to new technologies and progressively enhance our website as time goes on.

Apart from changing the layout, there is a lot more to responsive design. We can go beyond the viewing size of the device and can focus on the functionality or capabilities of a device. In cases, where our website uses hover functionality but we need to change it for touch screen devices that do not support hover functionality, we can serve different images or crop images on changing the screen resolution. Moreover, we can check whether we can trace the location of the device or whether the device is working on the Internet, or WIFI, and many more.

How responsive design works

The layout of a web page depends on or we can say is controlled abstractly by the following web languages:

- HTML
- CSS
- JavaScript

HTML describes what the content is, CSS is responsible for how the content looks, and with JavaScript we can do some really cool things, such as fallback mechanism. The website is designed to work for various screen sizes and devices which adapts and changes itself depending on the conditions using content first approach. This is achieved by using media queries that allow us to have specific CSS, used for custom fitting of layouts according to our need. We will look into media queries later in the chapter.

Screen resolutions

Different devices have different screen resolutions in landscape and in portrait mode. Here are some devices and device-supported screen resolutions in landscape as well as in portrait view:

Devices	Portrait View	Landscape View
iPhone 3G/3GS	320 x 480	480 x 320
Samsung Galaxy S Duos	480 x 800	800 x 480
iPhone 4	640 x 960	960 x 640
iPad	768 x 1024	1024 x 768

Devices	Resolutions
Most Netbooks	1024 x 600
MacBook Air 08	1280 x 800
Some Laptops	1366 x 768
MacBook Pro 15"	1440 x 900

Apart from these resolutions, today's latest devices, such as Samsung Galaxy S4 or iPhone 5, have very high resolutions in mobile device segment.

Viewport

Metadata is data (information) about data. The `<meta>` tag provides metadata about the HTML document. Metadata will not be displayed on the page, but will be machine parseable.

Meta elements are typically used to specify page description, keywords, author of the document last modified, and other metadata.

The metadata can be used by browsers (how to display content or reload page), search engines (keywords), or other web services.

For responsive design, to set the viewport width and initial scale on mobile devices, the following `<meta>` tag is generally used. In spite of responsive design, we can use this tag for non-responsive design too before we finalize our fit or restart approach. In fact, if we are building a responsive website or any mobile website, we still want this following tag:

```
<meta name="viewport" content="width=device-width, initial-scale=1.0">
```

Media queries

Media queries are CSS3 modules which allow content to adapt to various screen resolutions, such as smartphones, tablets, and high definition screens.

To deliver different styles to different devices, media queries are an excellent way to achieve this, providing the best experience for each type of user. As a part of the CSS3 specification, media queries expand the role of the `media` attribute that controls how the styles are applied.

A media query comprises of one or more expressions and type of media involving features that result in true or false. Moreover, relevant style sheet or style rules are applied, following the regular cascading rules when a media query is true.

The following snippet is a very simple example which applies when the device width is greater than 500 px:

```
@media screen and (min-width: 500px)
{
  /* some css here */
}
```

Media types

The device on which the linked document (external CSS) will be applied is specified by the `media` attribute's value. Using the `media` attribute inside a `<link>` element, a media type can be declared in the head of an HTML document. Within XML processing instructions, media types can be declared and the `@import` at-rule and the `@media` at-rule can be used.

Other media types defined by CSS2 are:

- `projection`: This is used for projected presentations such as slides
- `embossed`: This is used for braille printers
- `all`: This is used for all media type devices
- `aural`: This is used for sound and speech synthesizers
- `tv`: This is used for television type devices
- `screen`: This is used for computer screens
- `braille`: This is used for braille tactile feedback devices
- `handheld`: This is used for handheld or small devices

- `print`: This is used for printers
- `tty`: This is used for media using a fixed-pitch character grid, such as teletypes and terminals

An important feature of style sheets is that they specify how a document is to be presented on different media, such as on paper, on the screen with a speech synthesizer, or on a braille device.

We can apply different styles to a page view depending on which medium it is being used. With the help of a `media` attribute, internal and external style sheets can be associated with a media type.

Internal media query

These are the queries written within the HTML page inside the `<style>` tag.

Pros of internal media query are as follows:

- There is no need of extra HTTP requests
- This remains visible and not forgotten when updating the old one

Cons of internal media query are as follows:

- There is an increase in the file size in case user needs to download
- To make it work with older versions of the Internet Explorer browser, we have to use JavaScript

Syntax

The syntax for the internal media query is as follows:

```
body{
   background: blue;
}

@media screen and (max-width: 480px){
   body{
     background: black;
   }
}
```

Initially, it sets the background color to blue. But up to a maximum width of 480 pixels, it sets the background color to black that is overriding of CSS style.

External media query

These are the queries written and maintained in the separated file or in the external CSS file.

Pros of external media query are as follows:

- This is easy to keep and maintain CSS when extensively used
- Using conditional comments, we can use external media query with old versions of Internet Explorer
- For non-supporting browsers, the file size is smaller

Cons of external media query are as follows:

- An extra HTTP request is needed to apply it
- This can be easily forgotten in case of updating the old one

Extend the existing media part of the link element or the `@import` rule:

```
<link href="example.css" rel="stylesheet" media="only screen and (max-width:480px)">
@import url(example.css) only screen and (max-width:480px);
```

Media features

Media features resemble CSS properties syntactically as they have names and accept certain values, or we can say that they are the conditions with which we can customize our responsive design.

Some media features are listed in the following table:

Feature	Accepts min/max prefix	Value	Description
device-width	yes	length	Irrespective of the browser window's width, this determines the width of the device's entire screen.
device-height	yes	length	This determines the height of the device's screen.
orientation	no	portrait or landscape	This determines the orientation of the device. The two orientation modes are landscape and portrait.

Feature	Accepts min/max prefix	Value	Description
width	yes	length	This determines the width of the displayable area.
			It remains constant in most of the mobile browsers because of the inability of resizing the browser size, but with desktop computers, the width changes when the user resizes the browser.
height	yes	length	This determines the height of the display area.
grid	no	1 or 0	This detects whether the output device is bitmap or grid. Grid-based devices return a value of 1 and all other device return a value of 0.
device-aspect-ratio	yes	ratio	This determines the ratio of value of the device-width media to the device-height media.
resolution	yes	resolution	This determines the density of the pixels or resolution of the output device.
color	yes	integer	This determines the device's number of bits per color component. The value is zero when the device is not a color device.
color-index	yes	integer	In the color lookup table of the output device, this determines the number of entries.
monochrome	yes	integer	This determines the number of bits per pixel in a monochrome frame buffer. This value is 0 for non-monochrome devices.
aspect-ratio	yes	ratio	This determines the ratio of value of the width media to the height media.
scan	no	progressive or interlace	Progressive or interlaced, this determines the scanning process of TV.

Different screen resolutions

In this particular section, we will focus on the syntax for setting a minimum or maximum width of general and device-specific screen resolutions. We will also discuss the orientation of the device.

We cannot set the browser's screen resolution with CSS.

Small screen devices

We can use the following code for small screen devices with a maximum device width of 480 px:

```
@media screen and (max-device-width: 480px)
{
  /* some CSS here */
}
```

Any CSS written inside the media query will be applied to devices with a width of 480 px or less. The purpose of using `max-device-width` instead of `device-width` is that `device-width` refers to the width of the device but does not refer to the width of the display area. In case of browsers where we can change the resolution can be changed if the user resizes it, so we used `max-device-width`.

Until and unless, the screen resolution or browser size (in cases where we can change the browser size) is 480 px or less, the media query does not take effect, which basically leaves us for mobile devices.

High resolution displays of Apple mobile devices

Apple introduced devices, such as the iPhone 5 and iPad 3. In their earlier devices, such as the iPhone 4 and 4S, they had introduced an idea of retina display. In retina display, the screen resolution of the device gets doubled. Apple supports a proprietary property called `-webkit-device-pixel-ratio` that returns the pixel density of the device. So, this device returns a value of 2.

For high resolution devices

We can use the following code for general Apple devices with a high resolution:

```
@media screen and (-webkit-min-device-pixel-ratio: 1.5)
{
  /* some css here */
}
```

For small screen high resolution devices

We can use the following code for small screen with high resolution devices, such as the iPhone 4:

```
@media screen and (-webkit-min-device-pixel-ratio: 2)
  and (max-device-width: 480px)
{
  /* some css here */
}
```

For large screen high resolution devices

We can use the following code for large screen with high resolution devices, such as the iPad 3:

```
@media screen and (-webkit-min-device-pixel-ratio: 2)
  and (min-device-width: 768px)
{
  /* some css here */
}
```

Because of high resolution, images are the most popular choice which can be optimized for retina displays as depending on the device; we can serve two different versions of an image. For retina displays, we double the size and resolution of the original image but when we use this image, we apply a constraint to its dimensions to be the same as the original one and allow retina devices to show two pixels for every pixel shown as a result we get a super clear image.

The following code is an example for a background image:

```
normal background for the browsers:

div#featuredbox{
  width: 80%;
  height: 350px;
  background: url(normal_background.jpg) center no-repeat;
}

retina devices with larger screens:

@media screen and (-webkit-min-device-pixel-ratio: 2)
  and (min-device-width: 768px){
div#featuredbox{
  -webkit-background-size: 50% auto;
  background: url(highresolution_background.jpg)
    center no-repeat;
  }
}
```

In the preceding example, `-webkit-background-size: 50% auto;` shrinks the image by 50 percent of its actual dimensions, which matches that of the original image. `background: url(highresolution_background.jpg) center no-repeat;` is the high resolution image which doubles the size or resolution of the original image.

Devices in landscape and portrait modes

Apart from dealing with screen sizes, tackling the orientation of a device before media queries was hectic, but the introduction of media queries has eased the life of developers:

```
@media screen and (orientation: portrait)
{
  /* some CSS here */
}
```

The preceding code will target all devices whose screen height is longer than its width. Going further in situations where the user might be using a small screen device where orientation matters.

Small screen devices in portrait mode only

We can use the following code for screens with a maximum width of 480 px resolution for portrait mode:

```
@media screen and (max-device-width: 480px)
  and (orientation: portrait)
{
  /* some CSS here */
}
```

Small screen devices in landscape mode only

We can use the following code for screens with a maximum width of 640 px resolution for landscape mode:

```
@media screen and (max-device-width: 640px)
  and (orientation: landscape)
{
  /* some CSS here */
}
```

Of the technical pillars of responsive web design, media queries are the best established and supported. Additionally, they offer a solid return on investment from a design perspective and can be applied to existing applications to great effect.

Fluid grids

A fluid is a substance that continually changes its form and shape accordingly when applied under a shear stress.

In terms of web design, fluid refers to our design that we adapt and shear stress refers to the screen resolution according to which the fluid components adjust. Components in fluid designs adapt the environment or the screen resolution and flow accordingly.

For responsive design, we can say that this is a combination of a number of elements in which one is fluid grids and another is the use of media queries to load CSS, depending on the size of the screen along with its types; so we can say that fluid grids are not exactly responsive designs in themselves.

To keep the layout clean and to easily divide the grid into a specific number of columns, the maximum layout size is defined in the fluid grids. Instead of pixel-based dimensions, each element inside the grid is designed with proportional widths and heights so that they adapt according to the parent container. Elements will adjust their width and height according to the container in which they reside whenever the screen size is changed.

As fluid grids flow naturally along with the change in dimensions, we have to perform limited adjustments for different screen sizes and device types. Whereas in case of adaptive grids, we have to define definite pixel-based dimensions and have to manually adjust the height and width of the element in device viewports. In fluid grids, we can adjust `max-width,` which has great importance, since nowadays mobile devices are more powerful, so a person may spend most of the time performing various tasks using the mobile device itself.

Fluid grid generators

Fluid grids are not easy, and creating them from scratch requires effort and time and is a tedious task. Since most of the grid frameworks come with advanced built-in features and have been tested across various major browsers, it is wise to choose an existing CSS grid framework or a grid generator as the base for our layout creation and designs. Some CSS grid systems and generators that we can use are:

- Fluid grid system
- Tiny fluid grid
- Fluid grids by calculator
- Fluid grids by bootstrap

Creating a grid with fluid columns is easy when we have a CSS framework, but all designs are not going to be straightforward. We might need to create columns and rows inside other columns and rows. Nested columns are columns contained within a parent column.

960 grid system

Starting with desktop as the primary focus, 960 grid system, which was designed by *Nathan Smith*, is quite good if you're looking for a desktop solution. Smith has more recently put in the effort to move the framework so that it adapts to mobile devices also.

This system provides a tool that includes CSS and JavaScript files for handling rapid prototyping and publishing, as well as templates for many popular design environments, such as Omnigraffle, Fireworks, Balsamiq, and Photoshop, in order to provide a single solution for both desktop and mobile devices.

960 grid system's attention to detail has inspired elastic and fluid variations, themes, and a system for adapting to our own CSS preferences. So, we can say that with this, we can set our preferred column number, column width, and gutterwidth — all while enjoying the benefit of the 960 grid system community.

Pros of 960 grid system are as follows:

- The creators also released other 960-based solutions, which eased its integration
- It features a custom CSS generator for customizing CSS accordingly
- 960 grid system has a lot of column configurations because it has a lot of divisors — 28 and higher

Cons of 960 grid system are as follows:

- It contains extra markup compared to another solution
- It has extra CSS file size compared to another solution
- It contains non-semantic class names

Bootstrap

Bootstrap is an HTML, CSS, and JavaScript framework that you can use as the base for creating websites or web applications. If you are involved in web development today, you must have heard of Twitter and GitHub, so when you hear of a framework that started life at Twitter and is the most popular repository on GitHub — beating even jQuery and Node.js — you'll gain some idea of the viral spread that has engulfed Bootstrap. In other words, it's a sleek, intuitive, and powerful frontend framework for faster and easier web development.

In short, it represents the drive behind responsive web design to enable developers to quickly release applications that hold the user's needs at the forefront.

As its responsive features are strong enough to stand alone, Bootstrap and its component library is one of the best solutions around. We can exploit the fluid nesting and offsetting that helps to set the framework apart from its peers. And while we will avoid taking advantage of the component styling for which many developers adopt Bootstrap, the ease with which the grid comes to life will make you keen to explore the framework's other features.

Pros of Bootstrap are as follows:

- It is fully customizable to include the only features we need to use
- It has been rigorously tested by developers
- Bootstrap is popular which means that developers are familiar with it
- It can help to do awesome stuff on the Web in a small amount of time

Cons of Bootstrap are as follows:

- It contains extra markup compared to another solution
- It has extra CSS file size compared to another solution
- It contains non-semantic class names are used in it

But using responsive CSS framework does not make our design responsive and moreover responsive design is not that simple. Unless we plan the design carefully, users will always face problems while browsing the content on smaller devices when we use fluid grids.

For perfect responsive design, we cannot depend on fluid grids, but we can adjust the fluid grids when necessary according to the design It user with the best browsing experience.

Adaptive images

Adaptive images load different types of images depending on the client-side adaption. They detect the user's device screen size and automatically create caches and deliver the appropriate type of HTML web page's images. Their basic purpose is to be used with responsive designs and to be combined with fluid image techniques. This is because our website is being viewed not only in smaller devices, but also devices that are slower and have lower bandwidth. So, particularly in these devices, our desktop-based images load slowly, which causes more user bandwidth, increases cost, and rendering of user interface takes time. All these problems are fixed by adaptive images.

Adaptive images follow an identical semantic and structural model for `<img>`, `<audio>`, or `<video>` elements. Moreover, the `<source>` element should have the `media` attribute that supports CSS3 media queries which add the respective elements rendered on the given device.

For example:

```
<imgsrc="header.png" width="480" height="240" alt="head"
  media= "handheld and (max-device-width: 480px)">
<source src= "header.png" type="image/png" media= "screen
  and (max-device-width: 800px)">
<source src= "header.png" type="image/png" media="screen
  and (max-device-width: 1600px)">
</img>
```

Features

Some of the features of adaptive images are as follows:

- It requires no mark-up changes
- It can be easily configured or customized
- It works fine with any CMS or works without CMS too
- It works easily on our existing website
- It follows the mobile-first philosophy which means design for mobile devices is covered first and then the larger screens.
- It is up and running within minutes

How it works

The steps to use adaptive images are as follows:

1. Add the `.htaccess` and `adaptive-images.php` files to the `document-root` folder.

2. We can download these files from `https://github.com/mattwilcox/Adaptive-Images`.

3. Add JavaScript to the `<head>` of the web page. Following is the JavaScript needed to be copied:

    ```
    <script>
    document.cookie='resolution='+Math.max(screen.width,
      screen.height)+'; path=/';
    </script>
    ```

4. For retina displays in Apple devices, we can use the following line:

```
<script>
document.cookie='resolution='+Math.max(screen.width,
   screen.height)+("devicePixelRatio" in window ?
   ","+devicePixelRatio : ",1")+'; path=/';
</script>
```

5. Add CSS media query values to $resolutions in the PHP file.

Customization

We can also change the default values by looking in the configuration section at the top of the PHP file (adaptive-images.php). The following points can be customized accordingly:

- We can set breakpoints to match CSS media queries
- We can change the name and location of the ai-cache folder
- We can change the quality of any generated JPG images saved
- We can set how long the browser should cache images for
- To help keep detail, we can sharpen rescaled images

Making our form responsive

In earlier chapters, from basics of the form we learned how to style, validate, and link our form with the database. In this section, we will learn how to make our form responsive.

We will re-use our form that we styled earlier and will see the new technique with which we can make our forms responsive.

The HTML code remains the same except that the following links are added to the <head> tag of the HTML page.

The following first line mentioned is the viewport <meta> tag:

```
<meta name="viewport" content="width=device-width, initial-
   scale=1.0" />
```

The second line is an external media query (explained for example). The code is maintained in a separate file but the media query is written in the <head> tag.

The following mentioned CSS file will get included and comes into action when the device screen resolution width is lower than or exactly 520 px, but as soon as the device resolution exceeds 520 px in width, the media query is no longer active.

In the styling, we have set the widths of the input text element to be 85 percent. We have also cleared the value of the form element radio button marked with the gender class to be none. Adjustments have been made in the styling of the **Submit** button with the font size set to 15 px and increasing the width to 23 percent. The class for date of birth, `div_dob`, is also cleared to none so that it falls under the same line in a sequential manner.

```
<link rel='stylesheet' media='screen and
  (max-width: 520px)' href='Css/Internal_MediaQuery.css' />
```

Here is the code written in CSS:

```css
#masteringhtml5_form .txtinput.textbox{
  width: 85%;
}
#masteringhtml5_form .txtinput{
  width: 85%;
}
#masteringhtml5_form .gender{
  float:none;
}
#masteringhtml5_form .gender span{
  font-size: 14px;
}
#masteringhtml5_form .txtinput.select{
  width: 97%;
}
#masteringhtml5_form .submit_btn{
  font-size:15px;
  width:23%;
  padding-top: 3px;
  padding-bottom: 3px;
}
#masteringhtml5_form .div_dob{
  width: 100%;
  float:none;
}
```

The preceding CSS code is already explained in *Chapter 3, Styling the Forms*, but the important point here is the internal media query that makes our form responsive for small screen devices.

The third line is the external media query file linked to the main HTML page:

```
<link href="Css/External_MediaQuery.css" rel="stylesheet" />
```

The following snippet is the CSS code that is maintained in a separate file:

```css
@media screen and (min-width: 1169px) and (max-width: 1255px){
  #masteringhtml5_form .txtinput{
    width:45.7%;
  }
  #masteringhtml5_form .dateinput{
    width: 90%;
  }
}

@media screen and (min-width: 957px) and (max-width: 1170px){
  #masteringhtml5_form .txtinput{
    width:44.7%;
  }
  #masteringhtml5_form .dateinput{
    width: 90%;
  }
#masteringhtml5_form .txtinput.textbox{
    width: 94%;
  }
}

@media screen and (min-width: 811px) and (max-width: 958px){
  #masteringhtml5_form .txtinput{
    width:43.7%;
  }
  #masteringhtml5_form .txtinput.textbox{
    width: 93.7%;
  }
  #masteringhtml5_form .dateinput{
    width: 88%;
  }
}

@media screen and (min-width: 707px) and (max-width: 812px){
  #masteringhtml5_form .txtinput{
    width:42.7%;
  }
  #masteringhtml5_form .txtinput.textbox{
    width: 92.7%;
  }
```

```
  #masteringhtml5_form .dateinput{
    width: 88%;
  }
}


@media screen and (min-width: 624px) and (max-width: 708px){
  #masteringhtml5_form .txtinput{
    width:41.7%;
  }
  #masteringhtml5_form .txtinput.textbox{
    width: 92%;
  }
  #masteringhtml5_form .dateinput{
    width: 86%;
  }
}


@media screen and (min-width: 567px) and (max-width: 625px){
  #masteringhtml5_form .txtinput{
    width:40.7%;
  }
  #masteringhtml5_form .txtinput.textbox{
    width: 90%;
  }
  #masteringhtml5_form .dateinput{
    width: 84%;
  }
}


@media screen and (min-width: 521px) and (max-width: 568px){
  #masteringhtml5_form .txtinput{
    width:39.7%;
  }
  #masteringhtml5_form .txtinput.select{
    width: 48.7%;
  }
  #masteringhtml5_form .txtinput.textbox{
    width: 90%;
  }
  #masteringhtml5_form .dateinput{
    width: 84%;
  }
}
```

In the preceding code, the media query is applied to the media type screen having the specific minimum width of the screen to the specific maximum width of the screen. We have overwritten the width of the classes `txtinput`, `select`, and `dateinput` that adjust according to the screen resolution. The elements reflow and adjust according to the specific screen resolution.

The following screenshots are of our form that we have made responsive. This responsive form responds for both web browser (changing the browser size) and various device screen resolutions.

For resolution 480 x 800, our form looks as the following screenshot:

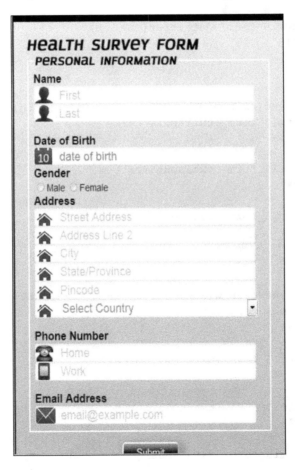

For resolution 768 x 1024, our form looks as the following screenshot:

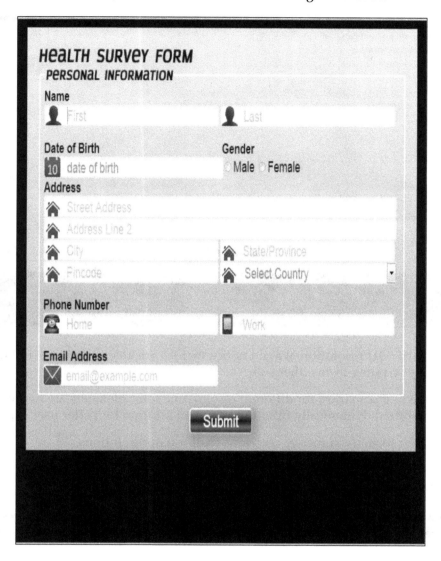

For resolution 1280 x 800, our form looks as the following screenshot:

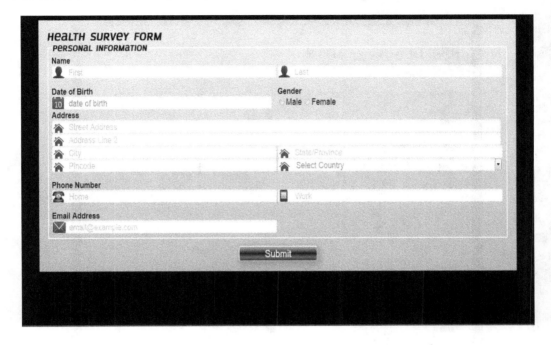

For each particular resolution, we can notice that we are able to view the full form without any scrolling from either side.

In the preceding scenarios, for different resolutions, some elements are resized and have been shifted dynamically from their original position for better user experience.

This way, our form dynamically responds to different resolutions.

Limitations

Mobile web design's new approach is responsive design, but one of the biggest challenges for web designers and their clients is finalizing the layout or wireframes as to how the website will look.

Some of the other challenges we need to overcome to build successful websites are:

- Responsive design takes more development time than building other websites
- Scaling images reduces image quality because scaling is based on screen size and not context
- On smaller devices, using navigation menus becomes a challenge

- Browser compatibility becomes an issue; because of older browsers, the support of media queries becomes limited
- Building complex websites becomes a tedious task with this technology
- Development cost is higher
- Response time of the website becomes slower because of the much larger size of the web page
- The loading time in mobile devices is increased while downloading the desktop content that is not even displayed

Guidelines

In this section, we will look at the guidelines for responsive design so as to make our forms more effective.

Some responsive design best practices are:

- Try to keep the content on the web page as minimum as possible for better responsive design.
- Always prioritize the content as you have a limitation on smaller screens.
- Try to use navigation as minimum as possible.
- Web pages must be effectively programmed and structured.
- Responsive design isn't for mobiles only. The scope of responsive design is not limited to mobiles or tablets; in fact, we should remember that people also use large 27-inch desktop screens.
- Always keep focus on browser compatibility.
- Keep the forms short; if long forms are used, add a **Save** button and navigate the user to the next page.
- Always maintain separate files for responsive design for easy maintenance of code.

Summary

In this chapter, we learned about responsive design. Along with this, we saw the advantages and the recommendations for responsive design.

We learned the various techniques with which we can make our forms responsive.

Then, with the help of code, we learned the practical implementation of responsive web forms by re-using the example we built in earlier chapters.

Lastly, we saw the best practices for making responsive forms more effective.

Index

A

adaptive images
about 116
customization 118
features 117
working 117
all, media types 107
angle value, gradients 68
aspect-ratio feature 110
aural, media types 107
autocomplete attribute 15
autofocus attribute 15, 77

B

background-attachment property 62
background-clip property
about 60
border-box value 60
content-box value 60
no-clip value 60
padding-box value 60
syntax 60
values 60
background-color property 62
background-origin property
about 61
border-box value 61
syntax 61
background-repeat property
about 62
content-box value 61
padding-box value 61
round value 62
space value 62
backgrounds
properties 60-62
background-size property
about 61, 77
contain value 62
cover value 62
length value 61
percentage value 61
syntax 61
values 61

Bootstrap
about 115
cons 116
pros 116
border-box value 60
border-image property
outset value 65
repeat value 65
slice value 64
source value 64
syntax 64
width value 64
border property
about 63
border-image property 64
border-radius property 63
border-radius property
% values 63
length values 63
syntax 63
box-shadow property
<blur> value 64
<color> value 64
<h-shadow>, <v-shadow> value 64
<spread> value 64
insect value 64
syntax 64
braille, media types 107

C

checkValidity method 37
client-side form validation
about 32
advantages 32
color feature 110
color-index feature 110
color type 10
color value, gradients 68
constraint validations
declaring 36
HTML5 APIs 36
content-box value 60
CSRF (Cross-Site Request Forgery) 94
CSS2
media types 107

form spoofing
about 92
expectations, setting 95
HTTP requests, forging 92, 93
one-time tokens 94, 95
submission, spoofing 93, 94
formtarget attribute 18
form validation
about 31
benefits 31
client-side form validation 32
server-side form validation 33

G

GET method 80
gradients
about 68
angle value 68
color value 68
syntax 68
grid feature 110

H

handheld, media types 107
hanging-punctuation property 66
height feature 110
high resolution displays
for high resolution devices 111
for large screen high resolution devices 112
for small screen high resolution devices 111
small screen devices, in landscape mode only 113
small screen devices, in portrait mode only 113
HTML5 constraint validation APIs
about 36
checkValidity method 37, 38
customError property 43
patternMismatch property 42
rangeOverflow property 44
rangeUnderflow property 45
setCustomValidity() method 38, 39
stepMismatch property 47
tooLong property 48
typeMismatch property 49
validationMessage attribute 41, 42

validity object 36
valid property 51
valueMissing property 50
willValidate attribute 40, 41
HTML5 form
advantages 9
building 20-29
HTML5 form validation
about 34
textbox validation, HTML5 <form> controls used 35
textbox validation, JavaScript used 34

I

internal media query
cons 108
pros 108
syntax 108

L

list attribute 16

M

max attribute 16, 53
maxlength attribute 53
media features
aspect-ratio 110
color 110
color-index 110
device-aspect-ratio 110
device-height 109
device-width 109
grid 110
height 110
monochrome 110
orientation 109
resolution 110
scan 110
width 110
media queries
about 107
media features 109
media types 107
media types
all 107

S

search type 12
scan feature 110
screen, media types 107
screen resolution
  small screen devices 111
selectors
  about 58
  [att$=val] 58
  [att^=val] 58
  [att:=val] 58
server
  form, linking to 95-102
server-side form validation
  about 33
  advantages 33
  disadvantages 33
setCustomValidity() method 38, 39
src font descriptor 67
step attribute 19, 53
stepMismatch property
  about 47
  validity.stepMismatch property 47, 48
Structured Query Language (SQL) 88
submit_btn class 78
Submit button 29

T

tel type 12
text-align-last property 66
Textarea 29
text effects
  about 65
  dateinput class 77
  heading class 77
  legend class 77
  radiobutton 77
  submit_btn class 78
  text-shadow property 65
  txtinput class 77
  word-wrap property 65
text-emphasis property 66
text-justify property 66
text-outline property 66
text-overflow property 66
text-shadow property

about 65
syntax 65
text-wrap property 66
time type 13
tooLong property
  about 48
  validity.tooLong property 48, 49
tty, media types 108
tv, media types 107
txtinput class 77
typeMismatch property
  about 49
  validity.typeMismatch property 49

U

unicode-range font descriptor 68
url type 13

V

validationMessage attribute 41, 42
validity.customError property 43
validity object 36
validity.patternMismatch attribute 42, 43
validity.rangeOverflow property 45
validity.rangeUnderflow property 46
validity.tooLong property 48
validity.typeMismatch property 49
validity.valid property 51, 53
validity.valueMissing property 50
valid property
  about 51
  validity.valid property 51, 52, 53
valueMissing property
  about 50
  validity.valueMissing property 50

W

web forms
  about 7, 8
  advantages 8
web forms, for CSS3 57, 58
website building
  limitations 124, 125
week type 13
width feature 110

Thank you for buying
Mastering HTML5 Forms

About Packt Publishing

Packt, pronounced 'packed', published its first book "*Mastering phpMyAdmin for Effective MySQL Management*" in April 2004 and subsequently continued to specialize in publishing highly focused books on specific technologies and solutions.

Our books and publications share the experiences of your fellow IT professionals in adapting and customizing today's systems, applications, and frameworks. Our solution based books give you the knowledge and power to customize the software and technologies you're using to get the job done. Packt books are more specific and less general than the IT books you have seen in the past. Our unique business model allows us to bring you more focused information, giving you more of what you need to know, and less of what you don't.

Packt is a modern, yet unique publishing company, which focuses on producing quality, cutting-edge books for communities of developers, administrators, and newbies alike. For more information, please visit our website: www.packtpub.com.

About Packt Open Source

In 2010, Packt launched two new brands, Packt Open Source and Packt Enterprise, in order to continue its focus on specialization. This book is part of the Packt Open Source brand, home to books published on software built around Open Source licences, and offering information to anybody from advanced developers to budding web designers. The Open Source brand also runs Packt's Open Source Royalty Scheme, by which Packt gives a royalty to each Open Source project about whose software a book is sold.

Writing for Packt

We welcome all inquiries from people who are interested in authoring. Book proposals should be sent to author@packtpub.com. If your book idea is still at an early stage and you would like to discuss it first before writing a formal book proposal, contact us; one of our commissioning editors will get in touch with you.

We're not just looking for published authors; if you have strong technical skills but no writing experience, our experienced editors can help you develop a writing career, or simply get some additional reward for your expertise.

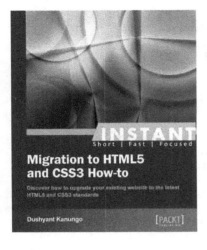

Instant Migration to HTML5 and CSS3 How-to [Instant]

ISBN: 978-1-84969-574-9   Paperback: 68 pages

Discover how to upgrade your existing website to the latest HTML5 and CSS3 standards

1. Learn something new in an Instant! A short, fast, focused guide delivering immediate results

2. Learn how to upgrade existing websites to HTML5 & CSS3 without changing appearance

3. Improve browser and mobile devices support for websites

4. Reduce the size of web pages by using the latest HTML5 elements and CSS3 features for faster, more-efficient websites

HTML5 Data and Services Cookbook

ISBN: 978-1-78355-928-2   Paperback: 480 pages

Over one hundred website building recipes utilizing all the modern HTML5 features and techniques!

1. Learn to effectively display lists and tables, draw charts, animate elements, and use modern techniques, such as templates and data-binding frameworks through simple and short examples

2. Examples utilizing modern HTML5 features, such as rich text editing, file manipulation, graphics drawing capabilities, real time communication

Please check **www.PacktPub.com** for information on our titles

open source*
community experience distilled

HTML5 Enterprise Application Development

HTML5 Enterprise Application Development

ISBN: 978-1-84968-568-9   Paperback: 332 pages

A step-by-step pratical introduction to HTML5 through the building of a real-world application, including common development practices

1. Learn the most useful HTML5 features by developing a real-world application

2. Detailed solutions to most common problems presented in an enterprise application development

3. Discover the most up-to-date development tips, tendencies, and trending libraries and tools

Getting Started with HTML5 WebSocket Programming

Getting Started with HTML5 WebSocket Programming

ISBN: 978-1-78216-696-2   Paperback: 110 pages

Develop and deploy your first secure and scalable real-time web application

1. Start real-time communication in your web applications

2. Create a feature-rich WebSocket chat application

3. Learn the step-by-step configuration of the server and clients

Please check **www.PacktPub.com** for information on our titles